GOSPEL OF LUKE
JOURNAL

THE NEW AMERICAN BIBLE

Thomas Nelson Publishers
Nashville

THE REVISED NEW TESTAMENT

NIHIL OBSTAT: Stephen J. Hartdegen, O.F.M., S.S.L.
Censor Deputatus
IMPRIMATUR: †James Cardinal Hickey, S.T.D., J.C.D.
Archbishop of Washington

August 27, 1986

Thomas Nelson Publishers is pleased to offer the *Gospel of Luke Journal* as an ideal tool for class, group, or individual study, and for personal reflection. Each Bible chapter in this volume is followed by several journaling pages where you may record your thoughts, prayers, and contemplations. Study notes and references related to the various chapters are found at the back of the book.

We trust that you will be enriched spiritually by your time in the Gospel of Luke, and we hope that you will consider expanding your study through the other journals in the series: the *Gospel of Matthew Journal,* the *Gospel of Mark Journal,* and the *Gospel of John Journal.* You may also want to purchase copies for family and friends. These journals make wonderful gifts of invitation to join the journey of faith through the Gospels!

The Books of the Old Testament and Their Abbreviations

Genesis	Gn	Proverbs	Prv
Exodus	Ex	Ecclesiastes	Eccl
Leviticus	Lv	Song of Songs	Sg
Numbers	Nm	Wisdom	Wis
Deuteronomy	Dt	Sirach	Sir
Joshua	Jos	Isaiah	Is
Judges	Jgs	Jeremiah	Jer
Ruth	Ru	Lamentations	Lam
1 Samuel	1 Sm	Baruch	Bar
2 Samuel	2 Sm	Ezekiel	Ez
1 Kings	1 Kgs	Daniel	Dn
2 Kings	2 Kgs	Hosea	Hos
1 Chronicles	1 Chr	Joel	Jl
2 Chronicles	2 Chr	Amos	Am
Ezra	Ezr	Obadiah	Ob
Nehemiah	Neh	Jonah	Jon
Tobit	Tb	Micah	Mi
Judith	Jdt	Nahum	Na
Esther	Est	Habakkuk	Hb
1 Maccabees	1 Mc	Zephaniah	Zep
2 Maccabees	2 Mc	Haggai	Hg
Job	Jb	Zechariah	Zec
Psalms	Ps(s)	Malachi	Mal

The Books of the New Testament and Their Abbreviations

Matthew	Mt	1 Timothy	1 Tm
Mark	Mk	2 Timothy	2 Tm
Luke	Lk	Titus	Ti
John	Jn	Philemon	Phlm
Acts of the Apostles	Acts	Hebrews	Heb
Romans	Rom	James	Jas
1 Corinthians	1 Cor	1 Peter	1 Pt
2 Corinthians	2 Cor	2 Peter	2 Pt
Galatians	Gal	1 John	1 Jn
Ephesians	Eph	2 John	2 Jn
Philippians	Phil	3 John	3 Jn
Colossians	Col	Jude	Jude
1 Thessalonians	1 Thes	Revelation	Rv
2 Thessalonians	2 Thes		

The Gospel According to Luke

The Gospel according to Luke is the first part of a two-volume work that continues the biblical history of God's dealings with humanity found in the Old Testament, showing how God's promises to Israel have been fulfilled in Jesus and how the salvation promised to Israel and accomplished by Jesus has been extended to the Gentiles. The stated purpose of the two volumes is to provide Theophilus and others like him with certainty—assurance—about earlier instruction they have received (1, 4). To accomplish his purpose, Luke shows that the preaching and teaching of the representatives of the early church are grounded in the preaching and teaching of Jesus, who during his historical ministry (Acts 1, 21–22) prepared his specially chosen followers and commissioned them to be witnesses to his resurrection and to all else that he did (Acts 10, 37–42). This continuity between the historical ministry of Jesus and the ministry of the apostles is Luke's way of guaranteeing the fidelity of the church's teaching to the teaching of Jesus.

Luke's story of Jesus and the church is dominated by a historical perspective. This history is first of all salvation history. God's divine plan for human salvation was accomplished during the period of Jesus, who through the events of his life (22, 22) fulfilled the Old Testament prophecies (4, 21; 18, 31; 22, 37; 24, 26–27.44), and this salvation is now extended to all humanity in the period of the church (Acts 4, 12). This salvation history, moreover, is a part of human history. Luke relates the story of Jesus and the church to events in contemporary Palestinian (1, 5; 3, 1–2; Acts 4, 6) and Roman (2, 1–2; 3, 1; Acts 11, 28; 18, 2.12) history for, as Paul says in Acts 26, 26, "this was not done in a corner." Finally, Luke relates the story of Jesus and the church to contemporaneous church history. Luke is concerned with presenting Christianity as a legitimate form of worship in the Roman world, a religion that is capable of meeting the spiritual needs of a world empire like that of Rome. To this end, Luke depicts the Roman governor Pilate declaring Jesus innocent of any wrongdoing three times (23, 4.14.22). At the same time Luke argues in Acts that Christianity is the logical development and proper fulfillment of Judaism and is therefore deserving of the same toleration and freedom traditionally accorded Judaism by Rome (Acts 13, 16–41; 23, 6–9; 24, 10–21; 26, 2–23).

The prominence given to the period of the church in the story has important consequences for Luke's interpretation of the teachings of Jesus. By presenting the time of the church as a distinct phase of salvation history, Luke accordingly shifts the early Christian emphasis away from the expectation of an imminent parousia to the day-to-day concerns of the Christian community in the world. He does this in the gospel by regularly emphasizing the words "each day" (9, 23; cf Mk 8, 34; Lk 11, 3; 16, 19; 19, 47) in the sayings of Jesus. Although Luke still believes the parousia to be a reality that will come unexpectedly (12, 38.45–46), he is more concerned with presenting the words and deeds of Jesus as guides for the conduct of Christian disciples in the interim period between the ascension and the parousia and with presenting Jesus himself as the model of Christian life and piety.

Throughout the gospel, Luke calls upon the Christian disciple to identify with the master Jesus, who is caring and tender toward the poor and lowly, the outcast, the sinner, and the afflicted, toward all those who recognize their dependence on God (4, 18; 6, 20–23; 7, 36–50; 14, 12–14; 15, 1–32; 16, 19–31; 18, 9–14; 19, 1–10; 21, 1–4), but who is severe toward the proud and self-righteous, and particularly toward those who place their material wealth before the service of God and his people (6, 24–26; 12, 13–21; 16, 13–15.19–31; 18, 9–14.15–25; cf 1, 50–53). No gospel writer is more concerned than Luke with the mercy and compassion of Jesus (7, 41–43; 10, 29–37; 13, 6–9; 15, 11–32). No gospel writer is more concerned with the role of the Spirit in the life of Jesus and the Christian disciple (1, 35.41; 2, 25–27; 4, 1.14.18; 10, 21; 11, 13; 24, 49), with the importance of prayer (3, 21; 5, 16; 6, 12; 9, 28; 11, 1–13; 18, 1–8), or with Jesus' concern for women (7, 11–17.36–50; 8, 2–3; 10, 38–42). While Jesus calls all humanity to repent (5, 32; 10, 13; 11, 32; 13, 1–5; 15, 7–10; 16, 30; 17, 3–4; 24, 47), he is particularly demanding of those who would be his disciples. Of them he demands absolute and total detachment from family and material possessions (9, 57–62; 12, 32–34; 14, 25–35). To all who respond in faith and repentance to the word Jesus preaches, he brings salvation (2, 30–32; 3, 6; 7, 50; 8, 48.50; 17, 19; 19, 9) and peace (2, 14; 7, 50; 8, 48; 19, 38.42) and life (10, 25–28; 18, 26–30).

Early Christian tradition, from the late second century on, identifies the author of this gospel and of the Acts of the Apostles as Luke, a Syrian from Antioch, who is mentioned in the New Testament in Col 4, 14, Phlm 1, 24, and 2 Tm 4, 11. The prologue of the gospel makes it clear that Luke is not part of the first generation of Christian disciples but is himself dependent upon the traditions he received from those who were eyewitnesses and ministers of the word (1, 2). His two-volume work marks him as someone who was highly literate both in the Old Testament traditions according to the Greek versions and in Hellenistic Greek writings.

Among the likely sources for the composition of this gospel (1, 3) were the Gospel of Mark, a written collection of sayings of Jesus known also to the author of the Gospel of Matthew (Q; see Introduction to Matthew), and other special traditions that were used by Luke alone among the gospel writers. Some hold that Luke used Mk only as a complementary source for rounding out the material he took from other traditions. Because of its dependence on the Gospel of Mark and because details in Luke's Gospel (13, 35a; 19, 43–44; 21, 20; 23, 28–31) imply that the author was acquainted with the destruction of the city of Jerusalem by the Romans in A.D. 70, the Gospel of Luke is dated by most scholars after that date; many propose A.D. 80–90 as the time of composition.

Luke's consistent substitution of Greek names for the Aramaic or Hebrew names occurring in his sources (e.g., 23, 33 // Mk 15, 22; 18, 41 // Mk 10, 51), his omission from the gospel of specifically Jewish Christian concerns found in his sources (e.g., Mk 7, 1–23), his interest in Gentile Christians (2, 30–32; 3, 6.38; 4, 16–30; 13, 28–30; 14, 15–24; 17, 11–19; 24, 47–48), and his incomplete knowledge of Palestinian geography, customs, and practices are among the characteristics of this gospel that suggest that Luke was a non-Palestinian writing to a non-Palestinian audience that was largely made up of Gentile Christians.

The principal divisions of the Gospel according to Luke are the following:

I: The Prologue (1, 1–4)
II: The Infancy Narrative (1, 5—2, 52)
III: The Preparation for the Public Ministry (3, 1—4, 13)
IV: The Ministry in Galilee (4, 14—9, 50)
V: The Journey to Jerusalem: Luke's Travel Narrative (9, 51—19, 27)
VI: The Teaching Ministry in Jerusalem (19, 28—21, 38)
VII: The Passion Narrative (22, 1—23, 56)
VIII: The Resurrection Narrative (24, 1–53)

Chapter 1

[1]*Since many have undertaken to compile a narrative of the events that have been fulfilled among us, [2]*just as those who were eyewitnesses from the beginning and ministers of the word have handed them down to us, [3]I too have decided, after investigating everything accurately anew, to write it down in an orderly sequence for you, most excellent Theophilus, [4]so that you may realize the certainty of the teachings you have received.

II: THE INFANCY NARRATIVE†

Announcement of the Birth of John. [5]*†In the days of Herod, King of Judea, there was a priest named Zechariah of the priestly division of Abijah; his wife was from the daughters of Aaron, and her name was Elizabeth. [6]Both were righteous in the eyes of God, observing all the commandments and ordinances of the Lord blamelessly. [7]*†But they had no child, because Elizabeth was barren and both were advanced in years. [8]Once when he was serving as priest in his division's turn before God, [9]*according to the practice of the priestly service, he was chosen by lot to enter the sanctuary of the Lord to burn incense. [10]Then, when the whole assembly of the people was praying outside at the hour of the incense offering, [11]the angel of the Lord appeared to him, standing at the right of the altar of incense. [12]Zechariah was troubled by what he saw, and fear came upon him. [13]*†But the angel said to him, "Do not be afraid, Zechariah, because your prayer has been heard. Your wife Elizabeth will bear you a son, and you shall name him John. [14]And you will have joy and gladness, and many will rejoice at his birth, [15]*†for he will be great in the sight of [the] Lord. He will drink neither wine nor strong drink. He will be filled with the holy Spirit even from his mother's womb, [16]and he will turn many of the children of Israel to the Lord their God. [17]*†He will go before him in the spirit and power of Elijah to turn the hearts of fathers toward children and the disobedient to the understanding of the righteous, to prepare a people fit for the Lord." [18]Then Zechariah said to the angel, "How shall I know this? For I am an old man, and my wife is advanced in years." [19]*†And the angel said to him in reply, "I am Gabriel, who stand before God. I was sent to speak to you and to announce to you this good news. [20]*†But now you will be speechless and unable to talk until the day these things take place, because you did not believe my words, which will be fulfilled at their proper time."

[21]Meanwhile the people were waiting for Zechariah and were amazed that he stayed so long in the sanctuary. [22]But when he came out, he was unable to speak to them, and they realized that he had seen a vision in the sanctuary. He was gesturing to them but remained mute. [23]Then, when his days of ministry were completed, he went home. [24]After this time his wife Elizabeth conceived, and she went into seclusion for five months, saying, [25]*"So has the Lord done for me at a time when he has seen fit to take away my disgrace before others."

Announcement of the Birth of Jesus.† [26]In the sixth month, the angel Gabriel was sent from God to a town of Galilee called Nazareth, [27]*to a virgin betrothed to a man named Joseph, of the house of David, and the virgin's name was Mary. [28]*And coming to her, he said, "Hail, favored one! The Lord is with you." [29]But she was greatly troubled at what was said and pondered what sort of greeting this might be. [30]Then the angel said to her, "Do not be afraid, Mary, for you have found favor with God. [31]*Behold, you will conceive in your womb and bear a son, and you shall name him Jesus. [32]*†He will be great and will be called Son of the Most High, and the Lord God will give him the throne of David his father, [33]*and he will rule over the house of Jacob forever, and of his kingdom there will be no end." [34]†But Mary said to the angel, "How can this be, since I have no relations with a man?" [35]*And the angel said to her in reply, "The holy Spirit will come upon you, and the power of the Most High will overshadow you. Therefore the child to be born will be called holy, the Son of God. [36]†And behold, Elizabeth, your relative, has also conceived a son in her old age, and this is the sixth month for her who was called barren; [37]*for nothing will be impossible for God." [38]Mary said, "Behold, I am the handmaid of the Lord. May it be done to me according to your word." Then the angel departed from her.

Mary Visits Elizabeth. [39]During those days Mary set out and traveled to the hill country in haste to a town of Judah, [40]where she entered the house of Zechariah and greeted Elizabeth. [41]*When Elizabeth heard Mary's greeting, the infant leaped in her womb, and Elizabeth, filled with the holy Spirit, [42]*cried out in a loud voice and said, "Most blessed are you among women, and blessed is the fruit of your womb. ⁴³†And how does this happen to me, that the mother of my Lord should come to me? ⁴⁴For at the moment the sound of your greeting reached my ears, the infant in my womb leaped for joy. ⁴⁵*†Blessed are you who believed that what was spoken to you by the Lord would be fulfilled."

The Canticle of Mary.† ⁴⁶*And Mary said:

"My soul proclaims the greatness of the Lord;
⁴⁷*   my spirit rejoices in God my savior.
⁴⁸* For he has looked upon his handmaid's lowliness;
        behold, from now on will all ages call me blessed.
⁴⁹* The Mighty One has done great things for me,
        and holy is his name.
⁵⁰* His mercy is from age to age
        to those who fear him.
⁵¹* He has shown might with his arm,
        dispersed the arrogant of mind and heart.
⁵²* He has thrown down the rulers from their thrones
        but lifted up the lowly.
⁵³* The hungry he has filled with good things;
        the rich he has sent away empty.
⁵⁴* He has helped Israel his servant,
        remembering his mercy,
⁵⁵* according to his promise to our fathers,
        to Abraham and to his descendants forever."

⁵⁶Mary remained with her about three months and then returned to her home.

The Birth of John.† ⁵⁷When the time arrived for Elizabeth to have her child she gave birth to a son. ⁵⁸*Her neighbors and relatives heard that the Lord had shown his great mercy toward her, and they rejoiced with her. ⁵⁹*†When they came on the eighth day to circumcise the child, they were going to call him Zechariah after his father, ⁶⁰*but his mother said in reply, "No. He will be called John." ⁶¹But they answered her, "There is no one among your relatives who has this name." ⁶²So they made signs, asking his father what he wished him to be called. ⁶³He asked for a tablet and wrote, "John is his name," and all were amazed. ⁶⁴*Immediately his mouth was opened, his tongue freed, and he spoke blessing God. ⁶⁵Then fear came upon all their neighbors, and all these matters were discussed throughout the hill country of Judea. ⁶⁶All who heard these things took them to heart, saying, "What, then, will this child be?" For surely the hand of the Lord was with him.

The Canticle of Zechariah. [67]Then Zechariah his father, filled with the holy Spirit, prophesied, saying:

[68]*†"Blessed be the Lord, the God of Israel,
    for he has visited and brought redemption to his people.
[69]*†He has raised up a horn for our salvation
    within the house of David his servant,
[70] even as he promised through the mouth of his holy prophets
    from of old:
[71]* salvation from our enemies and from the hand of all
    who hate us,
[72]* to show mercy to our fathers
    and to be mindful of his holy covenant
[73]* and of the oath he swore to Abraham our father,
    and to grant us that,
[74]   rescued from the hand of enemies,
  without fear we might worship him
[75]*   in holiness and righteousness
    before him all our days.
[76]*†And you, child, will be called prophet of the Most High,
    for you will go before the Lord to prepare his ways,
[77] to give his people knowledge of salvation
    through the forgiveness of their sins,
[78]*†because of the tender mercy of our God
    by which the daybreak from on high will visit us
[79] to shine on those who sit in darkness and death's shadow,
    to guide our feet into the path of peace."

[80]*The child grew and became strong in spirit, and he was in the desert until the day of his manifestation to Israel.

◆ Chapter 2 ◆

The Birth of Jesus.† ¹In those days a decree went out from Caesar Augustus that the whole world should be enrolled. ²This was the first enrollment, when Quirinius was governor of Syria. ³So all went to be enrolled, each to his own town. ⁴*And Joseph too went up from Galilee from the town of Nazareth to Judea, to the city of David that is called Bethlehem, because he was of the house and family of David, ⁵*to be enrolled with Mary, his betrothed, who was with child. ⁶While they were there, the time came for her to have her child, ⁷*†and she gave birth to her firstborn son. She wrapped him in swaddling clothes and laid him in a manger, because there was no room for them in the inn.

⁸†Now there were shepherds in that region living in the fields and keeping the night watch over their flock. ⁹*The angel of the Lord appeared to them and the glory of the Lord shone around them, and they were struck with great fear. ¹⁰The angel said to them, "Do not be afraid; for behold, I proclaim to you good news of great joy that will be for all the people. ¹¹*†For today in the city of David a savior has been born for you who is Messiah and Lord. ¹²And this will be a sign for you: you will find an infant wrapped in swaddling clothes and lying in a manger." ¹³And suddenly there was a multitude of the heavenly host with the angel, praising God and saying:

¹⁴*†"Glory to God in the highest
    and on earth peace to those on whom his favor rests."

The Visit of the Shepherds. ¹⁵When the angels went away from them to heaven, the shepherds said to one another, "Let us go, then, to Bethlehem to see this thing that has taken place, which the Lord has made known to us." ¹⁶So they went in haste and found Mary and Joseph, and the infant lying in the manger. ¹⁷When they saw this, they made known the message that had been told them about this child. ¹⁸All who heard it were amazed by what had been told them by the shepherds. ¹⁹And Mary kept all these things, reflecting on them in her heart. ²⁰Then the shepherds returned, glorifying and praising God for all they had heard and seen, just as it had been told to them.

The Circumcision and Naming of Jesus. ²¹*†When eight days were completed for his circumcision, he was named Jesus, the name given him by the angel before he was conceived in the womb.

The Presentation in the Temple.† ²²*†When the days were completed for their purification according to the law of Moses, they took him up to Jerusalem to present him to the Lord, ²³*just as it is written in the law of the Lord, "Every male that opens the womb shall be consecrated to the Lord," ²⁴and to offer the sacrifice of "a pair of turtledoves or two young pigeons," in accordance with the dictate in the law of the Lord.

²⁵†Now there was a man in Jerusalem whose name was Simeon. This man was righteous and devout, awaiting the consolation of Israel, and the holy Spirit was upon him. ²⁶It had been revealed to him by the holy Spirit that he should not see death before he had seen the Messiah of the Lord. ²⁷He came in the Spirit into the temple; and when the parents brought in the child Jesus to perform the custom of the law in regard to him, ²⁸he took him into his arms and blessed God, saying:

²⁹   "Now, Master, you may let your servant go
            in peace, according to your word,
³⁰*   for my eyes have seen your salvation,
³¹   which you prepared in sight of all the peoples,
³²*   a light for revelation to the Gentiles,
            and glory for your people Israel."

³³The child's father and mother were amazed at what was said about him; ³⁴*and Simeon blessed them and said to Mary his mother, "Behold, this child is destined for the fall and rise of many in Israel, and to be a sign that will be contradicted ³⁵†(and you yourself a sword will pierce) so that the thoughts of many hearts may be revealed." ³⁶There was also a prophetess, Anna, the daughter of Phanuel, of the tribe of Asher. She was advanced in years, having lived seven years with her husband after her marriage, ³⁷and then as a widow until she was eighty-four. She never left the temple, but worshiped night and day with fasting and prayer. ³⁸*And coming forward at that very time, she gave thanks to God and spoke about the child to all who were awaiting the redemption of Jerusalem.

The Return to Nazareth. ³⁹*When they had fulfilled all the prescriptions of the law of the Lord, they returned to Galilee, to their own town of Nazareth. ⁴⁰*The child grew and became strong, filled with wisdom; and the favor of God was upon him.

The Boy Jesus in the Temple.† ⁴¹*Each year his parents went to Jerusalem for the feast of Passover, ⁴²and when he was twelve years old, they went up according to festival custom. ⁴³After they had completed its days, as they were returning, the boy Jesus remained behind in Jerusalem, but his parents did not know it. ⁴⁴Thinking that he was in the caravan, they journeyed for a day and looked for him among their relatives and acquaintances, ⁴⁵but not finding him, they returned to Jerusalem to look for him. ⁴⁶After three days they found him in the temple, sitting in the midst of the teachers, listening to them and asking them questions, ⁴⁷and all who heard him were astounded at his understanding and his answers. ⁴⁸When his parents saw him, they were astonished, and his mother said to him, "Son, why have you done this to us? Your father and I have been looking for you with great anxiety." ⁴⁹†And he said to them, "Why were you looking for me? Did you not know that I must be in my Father's house?" ⁵⁰But they did not understand what he said to them. ⁵¹*He went down with them and came to Nazareth, and was obedient to them; and his mother kept all these things in her heart. ⁵²*And Jesus advanced [in] wisdom and age and favor before God and man.

❧ Chapter 3 ❧

The Preaching of John the Baptist.† ¹*†In the fifteenth year of the reign of Tiberius Caesar, when Pontius Pilate was governor of Judea, and Herod was tetrarch of Galilee, and his brother Philip tetrarch of the region of Ituraea and Trachonitis, and Lysanias was tetrarch of Abilene, ²*†during the high priesthood of Annas and Caiaphas, the word of God came to John the son of Zechariah in the desert. ³*†He went throughout [the] whole region of the Jordan, proclaiming a baptism of repentance for the forgiveness of sins, ⁴*†as it is written in the book of the words of the prophet Isaiah:

"A voice of one crying out in the desert:
'Prepare the way of the Lord,
 make straight his paths.
⁵ Every valley shall be filled
 and every mountain and hill shall be made low.
The winding roads shall be made straight,
 and the rough ways made smooth,
⁶* and all flesh shall see the salvation of God.' "

⁷*He said to the crowds who came out to be baptized by him, "You brood of vipers! Who warned you to flee from the coming wrath? ⁸*Produce good fruits as evidence of your repentance; and do not begin to say to yourselves, 'We have Abraham as our father,' for I tell you, God can raise up children to Abraham from these stones. ⁹*Even now the ax lies at the root of the trees. Therefore every tree that does not produce good fruit will be cut down and thrown into the fire."

¹⁰And the crowds asked him, "What then should we do?" ¹¹He said to them in reply, "Whoever has two cloaks should share with the person who has none. And whoever has food should do likewise." ¹²*Even tax collectors came to be baptized and they said to him, "Teacher, what should we do?" ¹³He answered them, "Stop collecting more than what is prescribed." ¹⁴Soldiers also asked him, "And what is it that we should do?" He told them, "Do not practice extortion, do not falsely accuse anyone, and be satisfied with your wages."

¹⁵*Now the people were filled with expectation, and all were asking in their hearts whether John might be the Messiah. ¹⁶*†John

answered them all, saying, "I am baptizing you with water, but one mightier than I is coming. I am not worthy to loosen the thongs of his sandals. He will baptize you with the holy Spirit and fire. [17]*†His winnowing fan is in his hand to clear his threshing floor and to gather the wheat into his barn, but the chaff he will burn with unquenchable fire." [18]Exhorting them in many other ways, he preached good news to the people. [19]*†Now Herod the tetrarch, who had been censured by him because of Herodias, his brother's wife, and because of all the evil deeds Herod had committed, [20]added still another to these by [also] putting John in prison.

The Baptism of Jesus.† [21]*†After all the people had been baptized and Jesus also had been baptized and was praying, heaven was opened [22]*†and the holy Spirit descended upon him in bodily form like a dove. And a voice came from heaven, "You are my beloved Son; with you I am well pleased."

The Genealogy of Jesus.† [23]*When Jesus began his ministry he was about thirty years of age. He was the son, as was thought, of Joseph, the son of Heli, [24]the son of Matthat, the son of Levi, the son of Melchi, the son of Jannai, the son of Joseph, [25]the son of Mattathias, the son of Amos, the son of Nahum, the son of Esli, the son of Naggai, [26]the son of Maath, the son of Mattathias, the son of Semein, the son of Josech, the son of Joda, [27]*the son of Joanan, the son of Rhesa, the son of Zerubbabel, the son of Shealtiel, the son of Neri, [28]the son of Melchi, the son of Addi, the son of Cosam, the son of Elmadam, the son of Er, [29]the son of Joshua, the son of Eliezer, the son of Jorim, the son of Matthat, the son of Levi, [30]the son of Simeon, the son of Judah, the son of Joseph, the son of Jonam, the son of Eliakim, [31]*†the son of Melea, the son of Menna, the son of Mattatha, the son of Nathan, the son of David, [32]the son of Jesse, the son of Obed, the son of Boaz, the son of Sala, the son of Nahshon, [33]*the son of Amminadab, the son of Admin, the son of Arni, the son of Hezron, the son of Perez, the son of Judah, [34]*the son of Jacob, the son of Isaac, the son of Abraham, the son of Terah, the son of Nahor, [35]the son of Serug, the son of Reu, the son of Peleg, the son of Eber, the son of Shelah, [36]*the son of Cainan, the son of Arphaxad, the son of Shem, the son of Noah, the son of Lamech, [37]the son of Methuselah, the son of Enoch, the son of Jared, the son of Mahalaleel, the son of Cainan, [38]the son of Enos, the son of Seth, the son of Adam, the son of God.

❧ Chapter 4 ❧

The Temptation of Jesus.† [1]*†Filled with the holy Spirit, Jesus returned from the Jordan and was led by the Spirit into the desert [2]*†for forty days, to be tempted by the devil. He ate nothing during those days, and when they were over he was hungry. [3]The devil said to him, "If you are the Son of God, command this stone to become bread." [4]*Jesus answered him, "It is written, 'One does not live by bread alone.'" [5]Then he took him up and showed him all the kingdoms of the world in a single instant. [6]*The devil said to him, "I shall give to you all this power and their glory; for it has been handed over to me, and I may give it to whomever I wish. [7]All this will be yours, if you worship me." [8]*Jesus said to him in reply, "It is written:

'You shall worship the Lord, your God,
  and him alone shall you serve.'"

[9]†Then he led him to Jerusalem, made him stand on the parapet of the temple, and said to him, "If you are the Son of God, throw yourself down from here, [10]*for it is written:

'He will command his angels concerning you,
  to guard you,'

[11]*and:

'With their hands they will support you,
  lest you dash your foot against a stone.'"

[12]*Jesus said to him in reply, "It also says, 'You shall not put the Lord, your God, to the test.'" [13]*†When the devil had finished every temptation, he departed from him for a time.

IV: THE MINISTRY IN GALILEE

The Beginning of the Galilean Ministry. [14]*†Jesus returned to Galilee in the power of the Spirit, and news of him spread throughout the whole region. [15]He taught in their synagogues and was praised by all.

The Rejection at Nazareth.† [16]*†He came to Nazareth, where he had grown up, and went according to his custom into the synagogue on the sabbath day. He stood up to read [17]and was handed a scroll of the prophet Isaiah. He unrolled the scroll and found the passage where it was written:

18*†"The Spirit of the Lord is upon me,
    because he has anointed me
        to bring glad tidings to the poor.
    He has sent me to proclaim liberty to captives
    and recovery of sight to the blind,
        to let the oppressed go free,
19   and to proclaim a year acceptable to the Lord."

20Rolling up the scroll, he handed it back to the attendant and sat down, and the eyes of all in the synagogue looked intently at him. 21†He said to them, "Today this scripture passage is fulfilled in your hearing." 22*And all spoke highly of him and were amazed at the gracious words that came from his mouth. They also asked, "Isn't this the son of Joseph?" 23†He said to them, "Surely you will quote me this proverb, 'Physician, cure yourself,' and say, 'Do here in your native place the things that we heard were done in Capernaum.' " 24And he said, "Amen, I say to you, no prophet is accepted in his own native place. 25*†Indeed, I tell you, there were many widows in Israel in the days of Elijah when the sky was closed for three and a half years and a severe famine spread over the entire land. 26*†It was to none of these that Elijah was sent, but only to a widow in Zarephath in the land of Sidon. 27*Again, there were many lepers in Israel during the time of Elisha the prophet; yet not one of them was cleansed, but only Naaman the Syrian." 28When the people in the synagogue heard this, they were all filled with fury. 29They rose up, drove him out of the town, and led him to the brow of the hill on which their town had been built, to hurl him down headlong. 30But he passed through the midst of them and went away.

The Cure of a Demoniac.† 31*Jesus then went down to Capernaum, a town of Galilee. He taught them on the sabbath, 32*and they were astonished at his teaching because he spoke with authority. 33*In the synagogue there was a man with the spirit of an unclean demon, and he cried out in a loud voice, 34*†"Ha! What have you to do with us, Jesus of Nazareth? Have you come to destroy us? I know who you are—the Holy One of God!" 35Jesus rebuked him and said, "Be quiet! Come out of him!" Then the demon threw the man down in front of them and came out of him without doing him any harm.

[36]They were all amazed and said to one another, "What is there about his word? For with authority and power he commands the unclean spirits, and they come out." [37]And news of him spread everywhere in the surrounding region.

The Cure of Simon's Mother-in-Law. [38]*†After he left the synagogue, he entered the house of Simon. Simon's mother-in-law was afflicted with a severe fever, and they interceded with him about her. [39]He stood over her, rebuked the fever, and it left her. She got up immediately and waited on them.

Other Healings. [40]*At sunset, all who had people sick with various diseases brought them to him. He laid his hands on each of them and cured them. [41]*†And demons also came out from many, shouting, "You are the Son of God." But he rebuked them and did not allow them to speak because they knew that he was the Messiah.

Jesus Leaves Capernaum. [42]*†At daybreak, Jesus left and went to a deserted place. The crowds went looking for him, and when they came to him, they tried to prevent him from leaving them. [43]*But he said to them, "To the other towns also I must proclaim the good news of the kingdom of God, because for this purpose I have been sent." [44]†And he was preaching in the synagogues of Judea.

≈Chapter 5≈

The Call of Simon the Fisherman.† ¹*While the crowd was pressing in on Jesus and listening to the word of God, he was standing by the Lake of Gennesaret. ²He saw two boats there alongside the lake; the fishermen had disembarked and were washing their nets. ³Getting into one of the boats, the one belonging to Simon, he asked him to put out a short distance from the shore. Then he sat down and taught the crowds from the boat. ⁴*After he had finished speaking, he said to Simon, "Put out into deep water and lower your nets for a catch." ⁵Simon said in reply, "Master, we have worked hard all night and have caught nothing, but at your command I will lower the nets." ⁶When they had done this, they caught a great number of fish and their nets were tearing. ⁷They signaled to their partners in the other boat to come to help them. They came and filled both boats so that they were in danger of sinking. ⁸When Simon Peter saw this, he fell at the knees of Jesus and said, "Depart from me, Lord, for I am a sinful man." ⁹For astonishment at the catch of fish they had made seized him and all those with him, ¹⁰*and likewise James and John, the sons of Zebedee, who were partners of Simon. Jesus said to Simon, "Do not be afraid; from now on you will be catching men." ¹¹*†When they brought their boats to the shore, they left everything and followed him.

The Cleansing of a Leper. ¹²*†Now there was a man full of leprosy in one of the towns where he was; and when he saw Jesus, he fell prostrate, pleaded with him, and said, "Lord, if you wish, you can make me clean." ¹³Jesus stretched out his hand, touched him, and said, "I do will it. Be made clean." And the leprosy left him immediately. ¹⁴*†Then he ordered him not to tell anyone, but "Go, show yourself to the priest and offer for your cleansing what Moses prescribed; that will be proof for them." ¹⁵The report about him spread all the more, and great crowds assembled to listen to him and to be cured of their ailments, ¹⁶*but he would withdraw to deserted places to pray.

The Healing of a Paralytic.† ¹⁷*†One day as Jesus was teaching, Pharisees and teachers of the law were sitting there who had come from every village of Galilee and Judea and Jerusalem, and the power of the Lord was with him for healing. ¹⁸And some men brought on a stretcher a man who was paralyzed; they were trying to bring him in and set [him] in his presence. [19]†But not finding a way to bring him in because of the crowd, they went up on the roof and lowered him on the stretcher through the tiles into the middle in front of Jesus. [20]†When he saw their faith, he said, "As for you, your sins are forgiven." [21]*†Then the scribes and Pharisees began to ask themselves, "Who is this who speaks blasphemies? Who but God alone can forgive sins?" [22]*Jesus knew their thoughts and said to them in reply, "What are you thinking in your hearts? [23]Which is easier, to say, 'Your sins are forgiven,' or to say, 'Rise and walk'? [24]*†But that you may know that the Son of Man has authority on earth to forgive sins"—he said to the man who was paralyzed, "I say to you, rise, pick up your stretcher, and go home." [25]He stood up immediately before them, picked up what he had been lying on, and went home, glorifying God. [26]Then astonishment seized them all and they glorified God, and, struck with awe, they said, "We have seen incredible things today."

The Call of Levi. [27]*After this he went out and saw a tax collector named Levi sitting at the customs post. He said to him, "Follow me." [28]†And leaving everything behind, he got up and followed him. [29]*Then Levi gave a great banquet for him in his house, and a large crowd of tax collectors and others were at table with them. [30]The Pharisees and their scribes complained to his disciples, saying, "Why do you eat and drink with tax collectors and sinners?" [31]Jesus said to them in reply, "Those who are healthy do not need a physician, but the sick do. [32]I have not come to call the righteous to repentance but sinners."

The Question about Fasting. [33]*And they said to him, "The disciples of John fast often and offer prayers, and the disciples of the Pharisees do the same; but yours eat and drink." [34]†Jesus answered them, "Can you make the wedding guests fast while the bridegroom is with them? [35]But the days will come, and when the bridegroom is taken away from them, then they will fast in those days." [36]†And he also told them a parable. "No one tears a piece from a new cloak to patch an old one. Otherwise, he will tear the new and the piece from it will not match the old cloak. [37]Likewise, no one pours new wine into old wineskins. Otherwise, the new wine will burst the skins, and it will be spilled, and the skins will be ruined. [38]Rather, new wine must be poured into fresh wineskins. [39]†[And] no one who has been drinking old wine desires new, for he says, 'The old is good.' "

Debates about the Sabbath.† ¹*While he was going through a field of grain on a sabbath, his disciples were picking the heads of grain, rubbing them in their hands, and eating them. ²Some Pharisees said, "Why are you doing what is unlawful on the sabbath?" ³*Jesus said to them in reply, "Have you not read what David did when he and those [who were] with him were hungry? ⁴*†[How] he went into the house of God, took the bread of offering, which only the priests could lawfully eat, ate of it, and shared it with his companions." ⁵Then he said to them, "The Son of Man is lord of the sabbath."

⁶*On another sabbath he went into the synagogue and taught, and there was a man there whose right hand was withered. ⁷*The scribes and the Pharisees watched him closely to see if he would cure on the sabbath so that they might discover a reason to accuse him. ⁸*But he realized their intentions and said to the man with the withered hand, "Come up and stand before us." And he rose and stood there. ⁹Then Jesus said to them, "I ask you, is it lawful to do good on the sabbath rather than to do evil, to save life rather than to destroy it?" ¹⁰Looking around at them all, he then said to him, "Stretch out your hand." He did so and his hand was restored. ¹¹But they became enraged and discussed together what they might do to Jesus.

The Mission of the Twelve.† ¹²*†In those days he departed to the mountain to pray, and he spent the night in prayer to God. ¹³†When day came, he called his disciples to himself, and from them he chose Twelve, whom he also named apostles: ¹⁴*†Simon, whom he named Peter, and his brother Andrew, James, John, Philip, Bartholomew, ¹⁵†Matthew, Thomas, James the son of Alphaeus, Simon who was called a Zealot, ¹⁶†and Judas the son of James, and Judas Iscariot, who became a traitor.

Ministering to a Great Multitude. ¹⁷*†And he came down with them and stood on a stretch of level ground. A great crowd of his disciples and a large number of the people from all Judea and Jerusalem and the coastal region of Tyre and Sidon ¹⁸came to hear him and to be healed of their diseases; and even those who were tormented by unclean spirits were cured. ¹⁹Everyone in the crowd sought to touch him because power came forth from him and healed them all.

Sermon on the Plain.† ²⁰*†And raising his eyes toward his disciples he said:

"Blessed are you who are poor,
   for the kingdom of God is yours.
21* Blessed are you who are now hungry,
      for you will be satisfied.
   Blessed are you who are now weeping,
      for you will laugh.
22* Blessed are you when people hate you,
      and when they exclude and insult you,
      and denounce your name as evil
      on account of the Son of Man.

23* Rejoice and leap for joy on that day! Behold, your reward will be great in heaven. For their ancestors treated the prophets in the same way.

24* But woe to you who are rich,
      for you have received your consolation.
25* But woe to you who are filled now,
      for you will be hungry.
   Woe to you who laugh now,
      for you will grieve and weep.
26* Woe to you when all speak well of you,
      for their ancestors treated the false prophets in this way.

Love of Enemies.† 27*"But to you who hear I say, love your enemies, do good to those who hate you, 28*bless those who curse you, pray for those who mistreat you. 29To the person who strikes you on one cheek, offer the other one as well, and from the person who takes your cloak, do not withhold even your tunic. 30Give to everyone who asks of you, and from the one who takes what is yours do not demand it back. 31*Do to others as you would have them do to you. 32For if you love those who love you, what credit is that to you? Even sinners love those who love them. 33And if you do good to those who do good to you, what credit is that to you? Even sinners do the same. 34*If you lend money to those from whom you expect repayment, what credit [is] that to you? Even sinners lend to sinners, and get back the same amount. 35*But rather, love your enemies and do good to them, and lend expecting nothing back; then your reward will be great and you will be children of the Most High, for he himself is kind to the ungrateful and the wicked. 36Be merciful, just as [also] your Father is merciful.

Judging Others.† 37*"Stop judging and you will not be judged.

Stop condemning and you will not be condemned. Forgive and you will be forgiven. 38*Give and gifts will be given to you; a good measure, packed together, shaken down, and overflowing, will be poured into your lap. For the measure with which you measure will in return be measured out to you." 39*And he told them a parable, "Can a blind person guide a blind person? Will not both fall into a pit? 40*No disciple is superior to the teacher; but when fully trained, every disciple will be like his teacher. 41Why do you notice the splinter in your brother's eye, but do not perceive the wooden beam in your own? 42How can you say to your brother, 'Brother, let me remove that splinter in your eye,' when you do not even notice the wooden beam in your own eye? You hypocrite! Remove the wooden beam from your eye first; then you will see clearly to remove the splinter in your brother's eye.

A Tree Known by Its Fruit.† 43*"A good tree does not bear rotten fruit, nor does a rotten tree bear good fruit. 44For every tree is known by its own fruit. For people do not pick figs from thornbushes, nor do they gather grapes from brambles. 45A good person out of the store of goodness in his heart produces good, but an evil person out of a store of evil produces evil; for from the fullness of the heart the mouth speaks.

The Two Foundations. 46*"Why do you call me, 'Lord, Lord,' but not do what I command? 47*†I will show you what someone is like who comes to me, listens to my words, and acts on them. 48That one is like a person building a house, who dug deeply and laid the foundation on rock; when the flood came, the river burst against that house but could not shake it because it had been well built. 49But the one who listens and does not act is like a person who built a house on the ground without a foundation. When the river burst against it, it collapsed at once and was completely destroyed."

Chapter 7

The Healing of a Centurion's Slave.† [1]*†When he had finished all his words to the people, he entered Capernaum. [2]†A centurion there had a slave who was ill and about to die, and he was valuable to him. [3]When he heard about Jesus, he sent elders of the Jews to him, asking him to come and save the life of his slave. [4]They approached Jesus and strongly urged him to come, saying, "He deserves to have you do this for him, [5]for he loves our nation and he built the synagogue for us." [6]†And Jesus went with them, but when he was only a short distance from the house, the centurion sent friends to tell him, "Lord, do not trouble yourself, for I am not worthy to have you enter under my roof. [7]Therefore, I did not consider myself worthy to come to you; but say the word and let my servant be healed. [8]For I too am a person subject to authority, with soldiers subject to me. And I say to one, 'Go,' and he goes; and to another, 'Come here,' and he comes; and to my slave, 'Do this,' and he does it." [9]When Jesus heard this he was amazed at him and, turning, said to the crowd following him, "I tell you, not even in Israel have I found such faith." [10]When the messengers returned to the house, they found the slave in good health.

Raising of the Widow's Son.† [11]*Soon afterward he journeyed to a city called Nain, and his disciples and a large crowd accompanied him. [12]*As he drew near to the gate of the city, a man who had died was being carried out, the only son of his mother, and she was a widow. A large crowd from the city was with her. [13]When the Lord saw her, he was moved with pity for her and said to her, "Do not weep." [14]He stepped forward and touched the coffin; at this the bearers halted, and he said, "Young man, I tell you, arise!" [15]*The dead man sat up and began to speak, and Jesus gave him to his mother. [16]*Fear seized them all, and they glorified God, exclaiming, "A great prophet has arisen in our midst," and "God has visited his people." [17]This report about him spread through the whole of Judea and in all the surrounding region.

The Messengers from John the Baptist.† [18]*The disciples of John told him about all these things. John summoned two of his disciples [19]*and sent them to the Lord to ask, "Are you the one who is to come, or should we look for another?" [20]When the men came to him, they said, "John the Baptist has sent us to you to ask, 'Are you the one who is to come, or should we look for another?' " [21]At that time he cured many of their diseases, sufferings, and evil spirits; he also granted sight to many who were blind. 22*And he said to them in reply, "Go and tell John what you have seen and heard: the blind regain their sight, the lame walk, lepers are cleansed, the deaf hear, the dead are raised, the poor have the good news proclaimed to them. 23†And blessed is the one who takes no offense at me."

Jesus' Testimony to John.† 24*When the messengers of John had left, Jesus began to speak to the crowds about John. "What did you go out to the desert to see—a reed swayed by the wind? 25Then what did you go out to see? Someone dressed in fine garments? Those who dress luxuriously and live sumptuously are found in royal palaces. 26*Then what did you go out to see? A prophet? Yes, I tell you, and more than a prophet. 27*This is the one about whom scripture says:

'Behold, I am sending my messenger ahead of you,
  he will prepare your way before you.'

28I tell you, among those born of women, no one is greater than John; yet the least in the kingdom of God is greater than he." 29*(All the people who listened, including the tax collectors, and who were baptized with the baptism of John, acknowledged the righteousness of God; 30but the Pharisees and scholars of the law, who were not baptized by him, rejected the plan of God for themselves.)

31*†"Then to what shall I compare the people of this generation? What are they like? 32They are like children who sit in the marketplace and call to one another,

'We played the flute for you, but you did not dance.
  We sang a dirge, but you did not weep.'

33For John the Baptist came neither eating food nor drinking wine, and you said, 'He is possessed by a demon.' 34*The Son of Man came eating and drinking and you said, 'Look, he is a glutton and a drunkard, a friend of tax collectors and sinners.' 35But wisdom is vindicated by all her children."

The Pardon of the Sinful Woman.† 36*†A Pharisee invited him to dine with him, and he entered the Pharisee's house and reclined at table. 37*Now there was a sinful woman in the city who learned that he was at table in the house of the Pharisee. Bringing an alabaster flask of ointment, 38she stood behind him at his feet weeping and began to bathe his feet with her tears. Then she wiped them with her hair, kissed them, and anointed them with the ointment. [39]When the Pharisee who had invited him saw this he said to himself, "If this man were a prophet, he would know who and what sort of woman this is who is touching him, that she is a sinner." [40]Jesus said to him in reply, "Simon, I have something to say to you." "Tell me, teacher," he said. [41]†"Two people were in debt to a certain creditor; one owed five hundred days' wages and the other owed fifty. [42]Since they were unable to repay the debt, he forgave it for both. Which of them will love him more?" [43]Simon said in reply, "The one, I suppose, whose larger debt was forgiven." He said to him, "You have judged rightly." [44]Then he turned to the woman and said to Simon, "Do you see this woman? When I entered your house, you did not give me water for my feet, but she has bathed them with her tears and wiped them with her hair. [45]You did not give me a kiss, but she has not ceased kissing my feet since the time I entered. [46]You did not anoint my head with oil, but she anointed my feet with ointment. [47]†So I tell you, her many sins have been forgiven; hence, she has shown great love. But the one to whom little is forgiven, loves little." [48]*He said to her, "Your sins are forgiven." [49]*The others at table said to themselves, "Who is this who even forgives sins?" [50]But he said to the woman, "Your faith has saved you; go in peace."

Chapter 8

Galilean Women Follow Jesus.† ¹*Afterward he journeyed from one town and village to another, preaching and proclaiming the good news of the kingdom of God. Accompanying him were the Twelve ²*and some women who had been cured of evil spirits and infirmities, Mary, called Magdalene, from whom seven demons had gone out, ³Joanna, the wife of Herod's steward Chuza, Susanna, and many others who provided for them out of their resources.

The Parable of the Sower.† ⁴*†When a large crowd gathered, with people from one town after another journeying to him, he spoke in a parable. ⁵"A sower went out to sow his seed. And as he sowed, some seed fell on the path and was trampled, and the birds of the sky ate it up. ⁶Some seed fell on rocky ground, and when it grew, it withered for lack of moisture. ⁷Some seed fell among thorns, and the thorns grew with it and choked it. ⁸*And some seed fell on good soil, and when it grew, it produced fruit a hundredfold." After saying this, he called out, "Whoever has ears to hear ought to hear."

The Purpose of the Parables. ⁹*Then his disciples asked him what the meaning of this parable might be. ¹⁰*He answered, "Knowledge of the mysteries of the kingdom of God has been granted to you; but to the rest, they are made known through parables so that 'they may look but not see, and hear but not understand.'

The Parable of the Sower Explained.† ¹¹*"This is the meaning of the parable. The seed is the word of God. ¹²Those on the path are the ones who have heard, but the devil comes and takes away the word from their hearts that they may not believe and be saved. ¹³Those on rocky ground are the ones who, when they hear, receive the word with joy, but they have no root; they believe only for a time and fall away in time of trial. ¹⁴As for the seed that fell among thorns, they are the ones who have heard, but as they go along, they are choked by the anxieties and riches and pleasures of life, and they fail to produce mature fruit. ¹⁵But as for the seed that fell on rich soil, they are the ones who, when they have heard the word, embrace it with a generous and good heart, and bear fruit through perseverance.

The Parable of the Lamp.† ¹⁶*"No one who lights a lamp conceals it with a vessel or sets it under a bed; rather, he places it on a lampstand so that those who enter may see the light. ¹⁷*For there is nothing hidden that will not become visible, and nothing secret that will not be known and come to light. ¹⁸*Take care, then, how you hear. To anyone who has, more will be given, and from the one who has not, even what he seems to have will be taken away."

Jesus and His Family. ¹⁹*†Then his mother and his brothers came to him but were unable to join him because of the crowd. ²⁰*He was told, "Your mother and your brothers are standing outside and they wish to see you." ²¹†He said to them in reply, "My mother and my brothers are those who hear the word of God and act on it."

The Calming of a Storm at Sea.† ²²*One day he got into a boat with his disciples and said to them, "Let us cross to the other side of the lake." So they set sail, ²³and while they were sailing he fell asleep. A squall blew over the lake, and they were taking in water and were in danger. ²⁴They came and woke him saying, "Master, master, we are perishing!" He awakened, rebuked the wind and the waves, and they subsided and there was a calm. ²⁵Then he asked them, "Where is your faith?" But they were filled with awe and amazed and said to one another, "Who then is this, who commands even the winds and the sea, and they obey him?"

The Healing of the Gerasene Demoniac. ²⁶*†Then they sailed to the territory of the Gerasenes, which is opposite Galilee. ²⁷When he came ashore a man from the town who was possessed by demons met him. For a long time he had not worn clothes; he did not live in a house, but lived among the tombs. ²⁸*When he saw Jesus, he cried out and fell down before him; in a loud voice he shouted, "What have you to do with me, Jesus, son of the Most High God? I beg you, do not torment me!" ²⁹For he had ordered the unclean spirit to come out of the man. (It had taken hold of him many times, and he used to be bound with chains and shackles as a restraint, but he would break his bonds and be driven by the demon into deserted places.) ³⁰†Then Jesus asked him, "What is your name?" He replied, "Legion," because many demons had entered him. ³¹†And they pleaded with him not to order them to depart to the abyss.

³²A herd of many swine was feeding there on the hillside, and they pleaded with him to allow them to enter those swine; and he let them. ³³The demons came out of the man and entered the swine, and the herd rushed down the steep bank into the lake and was drowned. ³⁴When the swineherds saw what had happened, they ran away and reported the incident in the town and throughout the countryside. ³⁵†People came out to see what had happened and, when they approached Jesus, they discovered the man from whom the demons had

come out sitting at his feet. He was clothed and in his right mind, and they were seized with fear. ³⁶Those who witnessed it told them how the possessed man had been saved. ³⁷The entire population of the region of the Gerasenes asked Jesus to leave them because they were seized with great fear. So he got into a boat and returned. ³⁸The man from whom the demons had come out begged to remain with him, but he sent him away, saying, ³⁹"Return home and recount what God has done for you." The man went off and proclaimed throughout the whole town what Jesus had done for him.

Jairus's Daughter and the Woman with a Hemorrhage.†

⁴⁰*When Jesus returned, the crowd welcomed him, for they were all waiting for him. ⁴¹And a man named Jairus, an official of the synagogue, came forward. He fell at the feet of Jesus and begged him to come to his house, ⁴²†because he had an only daughter, about twelve years old, and she was dying. As he went, the crowds almost crushed him. ⁴³†And a woman afflicted with hemorrhages for twelve years, who [had spent her whole livelihood on doctors and] was unable to be cured by anyone, ⁴⁴came up behind him and touched the tassel on his cloak. Immediately her bleeding stopped. ⁴⁵Jesus then asked, "Who touched me?" While all were denying it, Peter said, "Master, the crowds are pushing and pressing in upon you." ⁴⁶*But Jesus said, "Someone has touched me; for I know that power has gone out from me." ⁴⁷When the woman realized that she had not escaped notice, she came forward trembling. Falling down before him, she explained in the presence of all the people why she had touched him and how she had been healed immediately. ⁴⁸*He said to her, "Daughter, your faith has saved you; go in peace."

⁴⁹While he was still speaking, someone from the synagogue official's house arrived and said, "Your daughter is dead; do not trouble the teacher any longer." ⁵⁰On hearing this, Jesus answered him, "Do not be afraid; just have faith and she will be saved." ⁵¹When he arrived at the house he allowed no one to enter with him except Peter and John and James, and the child's father and mother. ⁵²*†All were weeping and mourning for her, when he said, "Do not weep any longer, for she is not dead, but sleeping." ⁵³And they ridiculed him, because they knew that she was dead. ⁵⁴But he took her by the hand and called to her, "Child, arise!" ⁵⁵Her breath returned and she immediately arose. He then directed that she should be given something to eat. ⁵⁶Her parents were astounded, and he instructed them to tell no one what had happened.

The Mission of the Twelve.† ¹*He summoned the Twelve and gave them power and authority over all demons and to cure diseases, ²and he sent them to proclaim the kingdom of God and to heal [the sick]. ³†He said to them, "Take nothing for the journey, neither walking stick, nor sack, nor food, nor money, and let no one take a second tunic. ⁴*Whatever house you enter, stay there and leave from there. ⁵*†And as for those who do not welcome you, when you leave that town, shake the dust from your feet in testimony against them." ⁶Then they set out and went from village to village proclaiming the good news and curing diseases everywhere.

Herod's Opinion of Jesus.† ⁷*†Herod the tetrarch heard about all that was happening, and he was greatly perplexed because some were saying, "John has been raised from the dead"; ⁸others were saying, "Elijah has appeared"; still others, "One of the ancient prophets has arisen." ⁹*†But Herod said, "John I beheaded. Who then is this about whom I hear such things?" And he kept trying to see him.

The Return of the Twelve and the Feeding of the Five Thousand. ¹⁰*When the apostles returned, they explained to him what they had done. He took them and withdrew in private to a town called Bethsaida. ¹¹The crowds, meanwhile, learned of this and followed him. He received them and spoke to them about the kingdom of God, and he healed those who needed to be cured. ¹²As the day was drawing to a close, the Twelve approached him and said, "Dismiss the crowd so that they can go to the surrounding villages and farms and find lodging and provisions; for we are in a deserted place here." ¹³*He said to them, "Give them some food yourselves." They replied, "Five loaves and two fish are all we have, unless we ourselves go and buy food for all these people." ¹⁴Now the men there numbered about five thousand. Then he said to his disciples, "Have them sit down in groups of [about] fifty." ¹⁵They did so and made them all sit down. ¹⁶*†Then taking the five loaves and the two fish, and looking up to heaven, he said the blessing over them, broke them, and gave them to the disciples to set before the crowd. ¹⁷They all ate and were satisfied. And when the leftover fragments were picked up, they filled twelve wicker baskets.

Peter's Confession about Jesus.† ¹⁸*†Once when Jesus was praying in solitude, and the disciples were with him, he asked them,

"Who do the crowds say that I am?" [19]*They said in reply, "John the Baptist; others, Elijah; still others, 'One of the ancient prophets has arisen.'" [20]†Then he said to them, "But who do you say that I am?" Peter said in reply, "The Messiah of God." [21]He rebuked them and directed them not to tell this to anyone.

The First Prediction of the Passion. [22]*He said, "The Son of Man must suffer greatly and be rejected by the elders, the chief priests, and the scribes, and be killed and on the third day be raised."

The Conditions of Discipleship. [23]*†Then he said to all, "If anyone wishes to come after me, he must deny himself and take up his cross daily and follow me. [24]*For whoever wishes to save his life will lose it, but whoever loses his life for my sake will save it. [25]What profit is there for one to gain the whole world yet lose or forfeit himself? [26]*Whoever is ashamed of me and of my words, the Son of Man will be ashamed of when he comes in his glory and in the glory of the Father and of the holy angels. [27]Truly I say to you, there are some standing here who will not taste death until they see the kingdom of God."

The Transfiguration of Jesus.† [28]*†About eight days after he said this, he took Peter, John, and James and went up the mountain to pray. [29]While he was praying his face changed in appearance and his clothing became dazzling white. [30]†And behold, two men were conversing with him, Moses and Elijah, [31]*†who appeared in glory and spoke of his exodus that he was going to accomplish in Jerusalem. [32]*†Peter and his companions had been overcome by sleep, but becoming fully awake, they saw his glory and the two men standing with him. [33]†As they were about to part from him, Peter said to Jesus, "Master, it is good that we are here; let us make three tents, one for you, one for Moses, and one for Elijah." But he did not know what he was saying. [34]†While he was still speaking, a cloud came and cast a shadow over them, and they became frightened when they entered the cloud. [35]*†Then from the cloud came a voice that said, "This is my chosen Son; listen to him." [36]†After the voice had spoken, Jesus was found alone. They fell silent and did not at that time tell anyone what they had seen.

The Healing of a Boy with a Demon.† [37]*On the next day when they came down from the mountain, a large crowd met him. [38]There was a man in the crowd who cried out, "Teacher, I beg you, look at my son; he is my only child. [39]For a spirit seizes him and he suddenly screams and it convulses him until he foams at the mouth t releases him only with difficulty, wearing him out. [40]I begged your disciples to cast it out but they could not." [41]Jesus said in reply, "O faithless and perverse generation, how long will I be with you and endure you? Bring your son here." [42]As he was coming forward, the demon threw him to the ground in a convulsion; but Jesus rebuked the unclean spirit, healed the boy, and returned him to his father. [43]*And all were astonished by the majesty of God.

The Second Prediction of the Passion. While they were all amazed at his every deed, he said to his disciples, [44]"Pay attention to what I am telling you. The Son of Man is to be handed over to men." [45]But they did not understand this saying; its meaning was hidden from them so that they should not understand it, and they were afraid to ask him about this saying.

The Greatest in the Kingdom.† [46]*An argument arose among the disciples about which of them was the greatest. [47]Jesus realized the intention of their hearts and took a child and placed it by his side [48]*and said to them, "Whoever receives this child in my name receives me, and whoever receives me receives the one who sent me. For the one who is least among all of you is the one who is the greatest."

Another Exorcist. [49]*Then John said in reply, "Master, we saw someone casting out demons in your name and we tried to prevent him because he does not follow in our company." [50]Jesus said to him, "Do not prevent him, for whoever is not against you is for you."

V: THE JOURNEY TO JERUSALEM: LUKE'S TRAVEL NARRATIVE†

Departure for Jerusalem; Samaritan Inhospitality.† [1]*†When the days for his being taken up were fulfilled, he resolutely determined to journey to Jerusalem, [52]*†and he sent messengers ahead of him. On the way they entered a Samaritan village to prepare for his reception there, [53]but they would not welcome him because the destination of his journey was Jerusalem. [54]*When the disciples James and John saw this they asked, "Lord, do you want us to call down fire from heaven to consume them?" [55]Jesus turned and rebuked them, [56]and they journeyed to another village.

The Would-be Followers of Jesus.† [57]*As they were proceeding on their journey someone said to him, "I will follow you wherever you go." [58]Jesus answered him, "Foxes have dens and birds of the sky

have nests, but the Son of Man has nowhere to rest his head." ⁵⁹And
to another he said, "Follow me." But he replied, "[Lord,] let me go
first and bury my father." ⁶⁰†But he answered him, "Let the dead bury
their dead. But you, go and proclaim the kingdom of God." ⁶¹*And
another said, "I will follow you, Lord, but first let me say farewell to
my family at home." ⁶²[To him] Jesus said, "No one who sets a hand
to the plow and looks to what was left behind is fit for the kingdom of
God."

Chapter 10

The Mission of the Seventy-two.† [1]*†After this the Lord appointed seventy[-two] others whom he sent ahead of him in pairs to every town and place he intended to visit. [2]*He said to them, "The harvest is abundant but the laborers are few; so ask the master of the harvest to send out laborers for his harvest. [3]*Go on your way; behold, I am sending you like lambs among wolves. [4]*†Carry no money bag, no sack, no sandals; and greet no one along the way. [5]†Into whatever house you enter, first say, 'Peace to this household.' [6]†If a peaceful person lives there, your peace will rest on him; but if not, it will return to you. [7]*Stay in the same house and eat and drink what is offered to you, for the laborer deserves his payment. Do not move about from one house to another. [8]*Whatever town you enter and they welcome you, eat what is set before you, [9]*cure the sick in it and say to them, 'The kingdom of God is at hand for you.' [10]*Whatever town you enter and they do not receive you, go out into the streets and say, [11]*'The dust of your town that clings to our feet, even that we shake off against you.' Yet know this: the kingdom of God is at hand. [12]*I tell you, it will be more tolerable for Sodom on that day than for that town.

Reproaches to Unrepentant Towns.† [13]*"Woe to you, Chorazin! Woe to you, Bethsaida! For if the mighty deeds done in your midst had been done in Tyre and Sidon, they would long ago have repented, sitting in sackcloth and ashes. [14]But it will be more tolerable for Tyre and Sidon at the judgment than for you. [15]*†And as for you, Capernaum, 'Will you be exalted to heaven? You will go down to the netherworld.' " [16]*Whoever listens to you listens to me. Whoever rejects you rejects me. And whoever rejects me rejects the one who sent me."

Return of the Seventy-two. [17]The seventy[-two] returned rejoicing, and said, "Lord, even the demons are subject to us because of your name." [18]*†Jesus said, "I have observed Satan fall like lightning from the sky. [19]*Behold, I have given you the power 'to tread upon serpents' and scorpions and upon the full force of the enemy and nothing will harm you. [20]*Nevertheless, do not rejoice because the spirits are subject to you, but rejoice because your names are written in heaven."

Praise of the Father. [21]*†At that very moment he rejoiced [in] the holy Spirit and said, "I give you praise, Father, Lord of heaven and earth, for although you have hidden these things from the wise and the learned you have revealed them to the childlike. Yes, Father, such has been your gracious will. [22]*All things have been handed over to me by my Father. No one knows who the Son is except the Father, and who the Father is except the Son and anyone to whom the Son wishes to reveal him."

The Privileges of Discipleship. [23]*Turning to the disciples in private he said, "Blessed are the eyes that see what you see. [24]For I say to you, many prophets and kings desired to see what you see, but did not see it, and to hear what you hear, but did not hear it."

The Greatest Commandment.† [25]*†There was a scholar of the law who stood up to test him and said, "Teacher, what must I do to inherit eternal life?" [26]Jesus said to him, "What is written in the law? How do you read it?" [27]*He said in reply, "You shall love the Lord your God, with all your heart, with all your being, with all your strength, and with all your mind, and your neighbor as yourself." [28]*He replied to him, "You have answered correctly; do this and you will live."

The Parable of the Good Samaritan. [29]But because he wished to justify himself, he said to Jesus, "And who is my neighbor?" [30]Jesus replied, "A man fell victim to robbers as he went down from Jerusalem to Jericho. They stripped and beat him and went off leaving him half-dead. [31]†A priest happened to be going down that road, but when he saw him, he passed by on the opposite side. [32]Likewise a Levite came to the place, and when he saw him, he passed by on the opposite side. [33]But a Samaritan traveler who came upon him was moved with compassion at the sight. [34]He approached the victim, poured oil and wine over his wounds and bandaged them. Then he lifted him up on his own animal, took him to an inn and cared for him. [35]The next day he took out two silver coins and gave them to the innkeeper with the instruction, 'Take care of him. If you spend more than what I have given you, I shall repay you on my way back.' [36]Which of these three, in your opinion, was neighbor to the robbers' victim?" [37]He answered, "The one who treated him with mercy." Jesus said to him, "Go and do likewise."

Martha and Mary.† [38]*As they continued their journey he entered a village where a woman whose name was Martha welcomed him. [39]†She had a sister named Mary [who] sat beside the Lord at his feet listening to him speak. [40]Martha, burdened with much serving, came to him and said, "Lord, do you not care that my sister has left me by myself to do the serving? Tell her to help me." [41]The Lord said to her in reply, "Martha, Martha, you are anxious and worried about many things. [42]†There is need of only one thing. Mary has chosen the better part and it will not be taken from her."

≈∝ Chapter 11 ∝≈

The Lord's Prayer.†[1]*†He was praying in a certain place, and when he had finished, one of his disciples said to him, "Lord, teach us to pray just as John taught his disciples." [2]†He said to them, "When you pray, say:

Father, hallowed be your name,
  your kingdom come.
[3]† Give us each day our daily bread
[4] and forgive us our sins
  for we ourselves forgive everyone in debt to us,
  and do not subject us to the final test."

Further Teachings on Prayer.[5]*And he said to them, "Suppose one of you has a friend to whom he goes at midnight and says, 'Friend, lend me three loaves of bread, [6]for a friend of mine has arrived at my house from a journey and I have nothing to offer him,' [7]and he says in reply from within, 'Do not bother me; the door has already been locked and my children and I are already in bed. I cannot get up to give you anything.' [8]I tell you, if he does not get up to give him the loaves because of their friendship, he will get up to give him whatever he needs because of his persistence.

The Answer to Prayer.[9]*"And I tell you, ask and you will receive; seek and you will find; knock and the door will be opened to you. [10]For everyone who asks, receives; and the one who seeks, finds; and to the one who knocks, the door will be opened. [11]What father among you would hand his son a snake when he asks for a fish? [12]Or hand him a scorpion when he asks for an egg? [13]†If you then, who are wicked, know how to give good gifts to your children, how much more will the Father in heaven give the holy Spirit to those who ask him?"

Jesus and Beelzebul.[14]*He was driving out a demon [that was] mute, and when the demon had gone out, the mute person spoke and the crowds were amazed. [15]*Some of them said, "By the power of Beelzebul, the prince of demons, he drives out demons." [16]*Others, to test him, asked him for a sign from heaven. [17]But he knew their thoughts and said to them, "Every kingdom divided against itself will be laid waste and house will fall against house. [18]And if Satan is divided against himself, how will his kingdom stand? For you say that it is by Beelzebul that I drive out demons. ¹⁹†If I, then, drive out demons by Beelzebul, by whom do your own people drive them out? Therefore they will be your judges. ²⁰*But if it is by the finger of God that [I] drive out demons, then the kingdom of God has come upon you. ²¹When a strong man fully armed guards his palace, his possessions are safe. ²²†But when one stronger than he attacks and overcomes him, he takes away the armor on which he relied and distributes the spoils. ²³*Whoever is not with me is against me, and whoever does not gather with me scatters.

The Return of the Unclean Spirit.²⁴*"When an unclean spirit goes out of someone, it roams through arid regions searching for rest but, finding none, it says, 'I shall return to my home from which I came.' ²⁵But upon returning, it finds it swept clean and put in order. ²⁶*Then it goes and brings back seven other spirits more wicked than itself who move in and dwell there, and the last condition of that person is worse than the first."

True Blessedness.† ²⁷*While he was speaking, a woman from the crowd called out and said to him, "Blessed is the womb that carried you and the breasts at which you nursed." ²⁸He replied, "Rather, blessed are those who hear the word of God and observe it."

The Demand for a Sign.† ²⁹*While still more people gathered in the crowd, he said to them, "This generation is an evil generation; it seeks a sign, but no sign will be given it, except the sign of Jonah. ³⁰Just as Jonah became a sign to the Ninevites, so will the Son of Man be to this generation. ³¹*At the judgment the queen of the south will rise with the men of this generation and she will condemn them, because she came from the ends of the earth to hear the wisdom of Solomon, and there is something greater than Solomon here. ³²*At the judgment the men of Nineveh will arise with this generation and condemn it, because at the preaching of Jonah they repented, and there is something greater than Jonah here.

The Simile of Light.³³*"No one who lights a lamp hides it away or places it [under a bushel basket], but on a lampstand so that those who enter might see the light. ³⁴*The lamp of the body is your eye. When your eye is sound, then your whole body is filled with light, but when it is bad, then your body is in darkness. ³⁵Take care, then, that the light in you not become darkness. ³⁶If your whole body is full of light, and no part of it is in darkness, then it will be as full of light as a lamp illuminating you with its brightness."

Denunciation of the Pharisees and Scholars of the Law.†

37*After he had spoken, a Pharisee invited him to dine at his home. He entered and reclined at table to eat. 38*The Pharisee was amazed to see that he did not observe the prescribed washing before the meal. 39*The Lord said to him, "Oh you Pharisees! Although you cleanse the outside of the cup and the dish, inside you are filled with plunder and evil. 40You fools! Did not the maker of the outside also make the inside? 41But as to what is within, give alms, and behold, everything will be clean for you. 42*Woe to you Pharisees! You pay tithes of mint and of rue and of every garden herb, but you pay no attention to judgment and to love for God. These you should have done, without overlooking the others. 43*Woe to you Pharisees! You love the seat of honor in synagogues and greetings in marketplaces. 44*†Woe to you! You are like unseen graves over which people unknowingly walk."

45*†Then one of the scholars of the law said to him in reply, "Teacher, by saying this you are insulting us too." 46And he said, "Woe also to you scholars of the law! You impose on people burdens hard to carry, but you yourselves do not lift one finger to touch them. 47*Woe to you! You build the memorials of the prophets whom your ancestors killed. 48Consequently, you bear witness and give consent to the deeds of your ancestors, for they killed them and you do the building. 49*†Therefore, the wisdom of God said, 'I will send to them prophets and apostles; some of them they will kill and persecute' 50in order that this generation might be charged with the blood of all the prophets shed since the foundation of the world, 51*†from the blood of Abel to the blood of Zechariah who died between the altar and the temple building. Yes, I tell you, this generation will be charged with their blood! 52*Woe to you, scholars of the law! You have taken away the key of knowledge. You yourselves did not enter and you stopped those trying to enter." 53*When he left, the scribes and Pharisees began to act with hostility toward him and to interrogate him about many things, 54*for they were plotting to catch him at something he might say.

The Leaven of the Pharisees. 1*†Meanwhile, so many people were crowding together that they were trampling one another underfoot. He began to speak, first to his disciples, "Beware of the leaven—that is, the hypocrisy—of the Pharisees.

Courage under Persecution.† 2*"There is nothing concealed that will not be revealed, nor secret that will not be known. 3Therefore whatever you have said in the darkness will be heard in the light, and what you have whispered behind closed doors will be proclaimed on the housetops. 4I tell you, my friends, do not be afraid of those who kill the body but after that can do no more. 5†I shall show you whom to fear. Be afraid of the one who after killing has the power to cast into Gehenna; yes, I tell you, be afraid of that one. 6†Are not five sparrows sold for two small coins? Yet not one of them has escaped the notice of God. 7*Even the hairs of your head have all been counted. Do not be afraid. You are worth more than many sparrows. 8I tell you, everyone who acknowledges me before others the Son of Man will acknowledge before the angels of God. 9*But whoever denies me before others will be denied before the angels of God.

Sayings about the holy Spirit.† 10*"Everyone who speaks a word against the Son of Man will be forgiven, but the one who blasphemes against the holy Spirit will not be forgiven. 11*When they take you before synagogues and before rulers and authorities, do not worry about how or what your defense will be or about what you are to say. 12For the holy Spirit will teach you at that moment what you should say."

Saying against Greed.† 13Someone in the crowd said to him, "Teacher, tell my brother to share the inheritance with me." 14*He replied to him, "Friend, who appointed me as your judge and arbitrator?" 15*Then he said to the crowd, "Take care to guard against all greed, for though one may be rich, one's life does not consist of possessions."

Parable of the Rich Fool. 16Then he told them a parable. "There was a rich man whose land produced a bountiful harvest. 17He asked himself, 'What shall I do, for I do not have space to store my harvest?' 18And he said, 'This is what I shall do: I shall tear down my barns and build larger ones. There I shall store all my grain and other goods 19*and I shall say to myself, "Now as for you, you have so many good things stored up for many years, rest, eat, drink, be merry!" ' ²⁰But God said to him, 'You fool, this night your life will be demanded of you; and the things you have prepared, to whom will they belong?' ²¹†Thus will it be for the one who stores up treasure for himself but is not rich in what matters to God."

Dependence on God. ²²*He said to [his] disciples, "Therefore I tell you, do not worry about your life and what you will eat, or about your body and what you will wear. ²³For life is more than food and the body more than clothing. ²⁴*Notice the ravens: they do not sow or reap; they have neither storehouse nor barn, yet God feeds them. How much more important are you than birds! ²⁵Can any of you by worrying add a moment to your lifespan? ²⁶If even the smallest things are beyond your control, why are you anxious about the rest? ²⁷*Notice how the flowers grow. They do not toil or spin. But I tell you, not even Solomon in all his splendor was dressed like one of them. ²⁸If God so clothes the grass in the field that grows today and is thrown into the oven tomorrow, will he not much more provide for you, O you of little faith? ²⁹As for you, do not seek what you are to eat and what you are to drink, and do not worry anymore. ³⁰All the nations of the world seek for these things, and your Father knows that you need them. ³¹Instead, seek his kingdom, and these other things will be given you besides. ³²*Do not be afraid any longer, little flock, for your Father is pleased to give you the kingdom. ³³*Sell your belongings and give alms. Provide money bags for yourselves that do not wear out, an inexhaustible treasure in heaven that no thief can reach nor moth destroy. ³⁴For where your treasure is, there also will your heart be.

Vigilant and Faithful Servants.† ³⁵*"Gird your loins and light your lamps ³⁶*and be like servants who await their master's return from a wedding, ready to open immediately when he comes and knocks. ³⁷Blessed are those servants whom the master finds vigilant on his arrival. Amen, I say to you, he will gird himself, have them recline at table, and proceed to wait on them. ³⁸And should he come in the second or third watch and find them prepared in this way, blessed are those servants. ³⁹*Be sure of this: if the master of the house had known the hour when the thief was coming, he would not have let his house be broken into. ⁴⁰You also must be prepared, for at an hour you do not expect, the Son of Man will come."

⁴¹Then Peter said, "Lord, is this parable meant for us or for everyone?" ⁴²And the Lord replied, "Who, then, is the faithful and prudent

steward whom the master will put in charge of his servants to distribute [the] food allowance at the proper time? [43]Blessed is that servant whom his master on arrival finds doing so. [44]Truly, I say to you, he will put him in charge of all his property. [45]†But if that servant says to himself, 'My master is delayed in coming,' and begins to beat the menservants and the maidservants, to eat and drink and get drunk, [46]then that servant's master will come on an unexpected day and at an unknown hour and will punish him severely and assign him a place with the unfaithful. [47]*That servant who knew his master's will but did not make preparations nor act in accord with his will shall be beaten severely; [48]and the servant who was ignorant of his master's will but acted in a way deserving of a severe beating shall be beaten only lightly. Much will be required of the person entrusted with much, and still more will be demanded of the person entrusted with more.

Jesus: A Cause of Division.† [49]"I have come to set the earth on fire, and how I wish it were already blazing! [50]*†There is a baptism with which I must be baptized, and how great is my anguish until it is accomplished! [51]*Do you think that I have come to establish peace on the earth? No, I tell you, but rather division. [52]From now on a household of five will be divided, three against two and two against three; [53]*a father will be divided against his son and a son against his father, a mother against her daughter and a daughter against her mother, a mother-in-law against her daughter-in-law and a daughter-in-law against her mother-in-law."

Signs of the Times. [54]*He also said to the crowds, "When you see [a] cloud rising in the west you say immediately that it is going to rain—and so it does; [55]and when you notice that the wind is blowing from the south you say that it is going to be hot—and so it is. [56]You hypocrites! You know how to interpret the appearance of the earth and the sky; why do you not know how to interpret the present time?

Settlement with an Opponent. [57]*"Why do you not judge for yourselves what is right? [58]If you are to go with your opponent before a magistrate, make an effort to settle the matter on the way; otherwise your opponent will turn you over to the judge, and the judge hand you over to the constable, and the constable throw you into prison. [59]†I say to you, you will not be released until you have paid the last penny."

Chapter 13

A Call to Repentance.† ¹†At that time some people who were present there told him about the Galileans whose blood Pilate had mingled with the blood of their sacrifices. ²*He said to them in reply, "Do you think that because these Galileans suffered in this way they were greater sinners than all other Galileans? ³*By no means! But I tell you, if you do not repent, you will all perish as they did! ⁴†Or those eighteen people who were killed when the tower at Siloam fell on them—do you think they were more guilty than everyone else who lived in Jerusalem? ⁵By no means! But I tell you, if you do not repent, you will all perish as they did!"

The Parable of the Barren Fig Tree.† ⁶*And he told them this parable: "There once was a person who had a fig tree planted in his orchard, and when he came in search of fruit on it but found none, ⁷he said to the gardener, 'For three years now I have come in search of fruit on this fig tree but have found none. [So] cut it down. Why should it exhaust the soil?' ⁸He said to him in reply, 'Sir, leave it for this year also, and I shall cultivate the ground around it and fertilize it; ⁹it may bear fruit in the future. If not you can cut it down.' "

Cure of a Crippled Woman on the Sabbath.† ¹⁰He was teaching in a synagogue on the sabbath. ¹¹And a woman was there who for eighteen years had been crippled by a spirit; she was bent over, completely incapable of standing erect. ¹²When Jesus saw her, he called to her and said, "Woman, you are set free of your infirmity." ¹³He laid his hands on her, and she at once stood up straight and glorified God. ¹⁴*But the leader of the synagogue, indignant that Jesus had cured on the sabbath, said to the crowd in reply, "There are six days when work should be done. Come on those days to be cured, not on the sabbath day." ¹⁵*†The Lord said to him in reply, "Hypocrites! Does not each one of you on the sabbath untie his ox or his ass from the manger and lead it out for watering? ¹⁶*†This daughter of Abraham, whom Satan has bound for eighteen years now, ought she not to have been set free on the sabbath day from this bondage?" ¹⁷When he said this, all his adversaries were humiliated; and the whole crowd rejoiced at all the splendid deeds done by him.

The Parable of the Mustard Seed.† ¹⁸*Then he said, "What is the kingdom of God like? To what can I compare it? ¹⁹*It is like a mustard seed that a person took and planted in the garden. When it was fully grown, it became a large bush and 'the birds of the sky dwelt in its branches.' "

The Parable of the Yeast. 20*Again he said, "To what shall I compare the kingdom of God? 21It is like yeast that a woman took and mixed [in] with three measures of wheat flour until the whole batch of dough was leavened."

The Narrow Door; Salvation and Rejection.† 22He passed through towns and villages, teaching as he went and making his way to Jerusalem. 23Someone asked him, "Lord, will only a few people be saved?" He answered them, 24*"Strive to enter through the narrow gate, for many, I tell you, will attempt to enter but will not be strong enough. 25*After the master of the house has arisen and locked the door, then will you stand outside knocking and saying, 'Lord, open the door for us.' He will say to you in reply, 'I do not know where you are from.' 26And you will say, 'We ate and drank in your company and you taught in our streets.' 27*Then he will say to you, 'I do not know where [you] are from. Depart from me, all you evildoers!' 28*And there will be wailing and grinding of teeth when you see Abraham, Isaac, and Jacob and all the prophets in the kingdom of God and you yourselves cast out. 29*And people will come from the east and the west and from the north and the south and will recline at table in the kingdom of God. 30*For behold, some are last who will be first, and some are first who will be last."

Herod's Desire to Kill Jesus. 31At that time some Pharisees came to him and said, "Go away, leave this area because Herod wants to kill you." 32†He replied, "Go and tell that fox, 'Behold, I cast out demons and I perform healings today and tomorrow, and on the third day I accomplish my purpose. 33*†Yet I must continue on my way today, tomorrow, and the following day, for it is impossible that a prophet should die outside of Jerusalem.'

The Lament over Jerusalem. 34*"Jerusalem, Jerusalem, you who kill the prophets and stone those sent to you, how many times I yearned to gather your children together as a hen gathers her brood under her wings, but you were unwilling! 35*Behold, your house will be abandoned. [But] I tell you, you will not see me until [the time comes when] you say, 'Blessed is he who comes in the name of the Lord.' "

Healing of the Man with Dropsy on the Sabbath.† ¹*On a sabbath he went to dine at the home of one of the leading Pharisees, and the people there were observing him carefully. ²†In front of him there was a man suffering from dropsy. ³*Jesus spoke to the scholars of the law and Pharisees in reply, asking, "Is it lawful to cure on the sabbath or not?" ⁴But they kept silent; so he took the man and, after he had healed him, dismissed him. ⁵*†Then he said to them, "Who among you, if your son or ox falls into a cistern, would not immediately pull him out on the sabbath day?" ⁶*But they were unable to answer his question.

Conduct of Invited Guests and Hosts.† ⁷*He told a parable to those who had been invited, noticing how they were choosing the places of honor at the table. ⁸*"When you are invited by someone to a wedding banquet, do not recline at table in the place of honor. A more distinguished guest than you may have been invited by him, ⁹and the host who invited both of you may approach you and say, 'Give your place to this man,' and then you would proceed with embarrassment to take the lowest place. ¹⁰Rather, when you are invited, go and take the lowest place so that when the host comes to you he may say, 'My friend, move up to a higher position.' Then you will enjoy the esteem of your companions at the table. ¹¹*For everyone who exalts himself will be humbled, but the one who humbles himself will be exalted." ¹²*Then he said to the host who invited him, "When you hold a lunch or a dinner, do not invite your friends or your brothers or your relatives or your wealthy neighbors, in case they may invite you back and you have repayment. ¹³Rather, when you hold a banquet, invite the poor, the crippled, the lame, the blind; ¹⁴*blessed indeed will you be because of their inability to repay you. For you will be repaid at the resurrection of the righteous."

The Parable of the Great Feast.† ¹⁵One of his fellow guests on hearing this said to him, "Blessed is the one who will dine in the kingdom of God." ¹⁶*He replied to him, "A man gave a great dinner to which he invited many. ¹⁷When the time for the dinner came, he dispatched his servant to say to those invited, 'Come, everything is now ready.' ¹⁸But one by one, they all began to excuse themselves. The first said to him, 'I have purchased a field and must go to examine it; I ask you, consider me excused.' ¹⁹And another said, 'I have purchased five yoke of oxen and am on my way to evaluate them; I ask you, consider me excused.' ²⁰And another said, 'I have just married a woman, and therefore I cannot come.' ²¹The servant went and reported this to his master. Then the master of the house in a rage commanded his servant, 'Go out quickly into the streets and alleys of the town and bring in here the poor and the crippled, the blind and the lame.' ²²The servant reported, 'Sir, your orders have been carried out and still there is room.' ²³The master then ordered the servant, 'Go out to the highways and hedgerows and make people come in that my home may be filled. ²⁴For, I tell you, none of those men who were invited will taste my dinner.' "

Sayings on Discipleship.† ²⁵Great crowds were traveling with him, and he turned and addressed them, ²⁶*†"If anyone comes to me without hating his father and mother, wife and children, brothers and sisters, and even his own life, he cannot be my disciple. ²⁷*Whoever does not carry his own cross and come after me cannot be my disciple. ²⁸Which of you wishing to construct a tower does not first sit down and calculate the cost to see if there is enough for its completion? ²⁹Otherwise, after laying the foundation and finding himself unable to finish the work the onlookers should laugh at him ³⁰and say, 'This one began to build but did not have the resources to finish.' ³¹Or what king marching into battle would not first sit down and decide whether with ten thousand troops he can successfully oppose another king advancing upon him with twenty thousand troops? ³²But if not, while he is still far away, he will send a delegation to ask for peace terms. ³³*In the same way, everyone of you who does not renounce all his possessions cannot be my disciple.

The Simile of Salt.† ³⁴*"Salt is good, but if salt itself loses its taste, with what can its flavor be restored? ³⁵*It is fit neither for the soil nor for the manure pile; it is thrown out. Whoever has ears to hear ought to hear."

The Parable of the Lost Sheep.† ¹*The tax collectors and sinners were all drawing near to listen to him, ²*but the Pharisees and scribes began to complain, saying, "This man welcomes sinners and eats with them." ³So to them he addressed this parable. ⁴*"What man among you having a hundred sheep and losing one of them would not leave the ninety-nine in the desert and go after the lost one until he finds it? ⁵And when he does find it, he sets it on his shoulders with great joy ⁶and, upon his arrival home, he calls together his friends and neighbors and says to them, 'Rejoice with me because I have found my lost sheep.' ⁷*I tell you, in just the same way there will be more joy in heaven over one sinner who repents than over ninety-nine righteous people who have no need of repentance.

The Parable of the Lost Coin. ⁸†"Or what woman having ten coins and losing one would not light a lamp and sweep the house, searching carefully until she finds it? ⁹And when she does find it, she calls together her friends and neighbors and says to them, 'Rejoice with me because I have found the coin that I lost.' ¹⁰In just the same way, I tell you, there will be rejoicing among the angels of God over one sinner who repents."

The Parable of the Lost Son. ¹¹Then he said, "A man had two sons, ¹²and the younger son said to his father, 'Father, give me the share of your estate that should come to me.' So the father divided the property between them. ¹³*After a few days, the younger son collected all his belongings and set off to a distant country where he squandered his inheritance on a life of dissipation. ¹⁴When he had freely spent everything, a severe famine struck that country, and he found himself in dire need. ¹⁵So he hired himself out to one of the local citizens who sent him to his farm to tend the swine. ¹⁶And he longed to eat his fill of the pods on which the swine fed, but nobody gave him any. ¹⁷Coming to his senses he thought, 'How many of my father's hired workers have more than enough food to eat, but here am I, dying from hunger. ¹⁸I shall get up and go to my father and I shall say to him, "Father, I have sinned against heaven and against you. ¹⁹I no longer deserve to be called your son; treat me as you would treat one of your hired workers." ' ²⁰So he got up and went back to his father. While he was still a long way off, his father caught sight of him, and was filled with compassion. He ran to his son, embraced him and kissed him. ²¹His son said to him, 'Father, I have sinned against heaven and against you; I no longer deserve to be called your son.' ²²But his father ordered his servants, 'Quickly bring the finest robe and put it on him; put a ring on his finger and sandals on his feet. ²³Take the fattened calf and slaughter it. Then let us celebrate with a feast, ²⁴because this son of mine was dead, and has come to life again; he was lost, and has been found.' Then the celebration began. ²⁵Now the older son had been out in the field and, on his way back, as he neared the house, he heard the sound of music and dancing. ²⁶He called one of the servants and asked what this might mean. ²⁷The servant said to him, 'Your brother has returned and your father has slaughtered the fattened calf because he has him back safe and sound.' ²⁸He became angry, and when he refused to enter the house, his father came out and pleaded with him. ²⁹He said to his father in reply, 'Look, all these years I served you and not once did I disobey your orders; yet you never gave me even a young goat to feast on with my friends. ³⁰But when your son returns who swallowed up your property with prostitutes, for him you slaughter the fattened calf.' ³¹He said to him, 'My son, you are here with me always; everything I have is yours. ³²But now we must celebrate and rejoice, because your brother was dead and has come to life again; he was lost and has been found.' "

❧ Chapter 16 ❧

The Parable of the Dishonest Steward.† ¹Then he also said to his disciples, "A rich man had a steward who was reported to him for squandering his property. ²He summoned him and said, 'What is this I hear about you? Prepare a full account of your stewardship, because you can no longer be my steward.' ³The steward said to himself, 'What shall I do, now that my master is taking the position of steward away from me? I am not strong enough to dig and I am ashamed to beg. ⁴I know what I shall do so that, when I am removed from the stewardship, they may welcome me into their homes.' ⁵He called in his master's debtors one by one. To the first he said, 'How much do you owe my master?' ⁶†He replied, 'One hundred measures of olive oil.' He said to him, 'Here is your promissory note. Sit down and quickly write one for fifty.' ⁷†Then to another he said, 'And you, how much do you owe?' He replied, 'One hundred kors of wheat.' He said to him, 'Here is your promissory note; write one for eighty.' ⁸*And the master commended that dishonest steward for acting prudently.

Application of the Parable.† "For the children of this world are more prudent in dealing with their own generation than are the children of light. ⁹*†I tell you, make friends for yourselves with dishonest wealth, so that when it fails, you will be welcomed into eternal dwellings. ¹⁰*†The person who is trustworthy in very small matters is also trustworthy in great ones; and the person who is dishonest in very small matters is also dishonest in great ones. ¹¹If, therefore, you are not trustworthy with dishonest wealth, who will trust you with true wealth? ¹²If you are not trustworthy with what belongs to another, who will give you what is yours? ¹³*†No servant can serve two masters. He will either hate one and love the other, or be devoted to one and despise the other. You cannot serve God and mammon."

A Saying against the Pharisees.† ¹⁴†The Pharisees, who loved money, heard all these things and sneered at him. ¹⁵*And he said to them, "You justify yourselves in the sight of others, but God knows your hearts; for what is of human esteem is an abomination in the sight of God.

Sayings about the Law. ¹⁶*†"The law and the prophets lasted until John; but from then on the kingdom of God is proclaimed, and everyone who enters does so with violence. ¹⁷*It is easier for heaven and earth to pass away than for the smallest part of a letter of the law to become invalid.

Sayings about Divorce. 18*"Everyone who divorces his wife and marries another commits adultery, and the one who marries a woman divorced from her husband commits adultery.

The Parable of the Rich Man and Lazarus.† 19†"There was a rich man who dressed in purple garments and fine linen and dined sumptuously each day. 20And lying at his door was a poor man named Lazarus, covered with sores, 21*who would gladly have eaten his fill of the scraps that fell from the rich man's table. Dogs even used to come and lick his sores. 22When the poor man died, he was carried away by angels to the bosom of Abraham. The rich man also died and was buried, 23†and from the netherworld, where he was in torment, he raised his eyes and saw Abraham far off and Lazarus at his side. 24And he cried out, 'Father Abraham, have pity on me. Send Lazarus to dip the tip of his finger in water and cool my tongue, for I am suffering torment in these flames.' 25*Abraham replied, 'My child, remember that you received what was good during your lifetime while Lazarus likewise received what was bad; but now he is comforted here, whereas you are tormented. 26Moreover, between us and you a great chasm is established to prevent anyone from crossing who might wish to go from our side to yours or from your side to ours.' 27He said, 'Then I beg you, father, send him to my father's house, 28for I have five brothers, so that he may warn them, lest they too come to this place of torment.' 29But Abraham replied, 'They have Moses and the prophets. Let them listen to them.' 30†He said, 'Oh no, father Abraham, but if someone from the dead goes to them, they will repent.' 31*Then Abraham said, 'If they will not listen to Moses and the prophets, neither will they be persuaded if someone should rise from the dead.' "

~_& Chapter 17 ~

Temptations to Sin. [1]*He said to his disciples, "Things that cause sin will inevitably occur, but woe to the person through whom they occur. [2]It would be better for him if a millstone were put around his neck and he be thrown into the sea than for him to cause one of these little ones to sin. [3]*†Be on your guard! If your brother sins, rebuke him; and if he repents, forgive him. [4]*And if he wrongs you seven times in one day and returns to you seven times saying, 'I am sorry,' you should forgive him."

Saying of Faith. [5]And the apostles said to the Lord, "Increase our faith." [6]*The Lord replied, "If you have faith the size of a mustard seed, you would say to [this] mulberry tree, 'Be uprooted and planted in the sea,' and it would obey you.

Attitude of a Servant.† [7]"Who among you would say to your servant who has just come in from plowing or tending sheep in the field, 'Come here immediately and take your place at table'? [8]Would he not rather say to him, 'Prepare something for me to eat. Put on your apron and wait on me while I eat and drink. You may eat and drink when I am finished'? [9]Is he grateful to that servant because he did what was commanded? [10]So should it be with you. When you have done all you have been commanded, say, 'We are unprofitable servants; we have done what we were obliged to do.' "

The Cleansing of Ten Lepers.† [11]*†As he continued his journey to Jerusalem, he traveled through Samaria and Galilee. [12]As he was entering a village, ten lepers met [him]. They stood at a distance from him [13]*and raised their voice, saying, "Jesus, Master! Have pity on us!" [14]*†And when he saw them, he said, "Go show yourselves to the priests." As they were going they were cleansed. [15]And one of them, realizing he had been healed, returned, glorifying God in a loud voice; [16]and he fell at the feet of Jesus and thanked him. He was a Samaritan. [17]Jesus said in reply, "Ten were cleansed, were they not? Where are the other nine? [18]Has none but this foreigner returned to give thanks to God?" [19]*Then he said to him, "Stand up and go; your faith has saved you."

The Coming of the Kingdom of God.† [20]*Asked by the Pharisees when the kingdom of God would come, he said in reply, "The coming of the kingdom of God cannot be observed, [21]*†and no one will announce, 'Look, here it is,' or, 'There it is.' For behold, the king-dom of God is among you."

The Day of the Son of Man. 22Then he said to his disciples, "The days will come when you will long to see one of the days of the Son of Man, but you will not see it. 23*There will be those who will say to you, 'Look, there he is,' [or] 'Look, here he is.' Do not go off, do not run in pursuit. 24*For just as lightning flashes and lights up the sky from one side to the other, so will the Son of Man be [in his day]. 25*But first he must suffer greatly and be rejected by this generation. 26*As it was in the days of Noah, so it will be in the days of the Son of Man; 27they were eating and drinking, marrying and giving in mar-riage up to the day that Noah entered the ark, and the flood came and destroyed them all. 28*Similarly, as it was in the days of Lot: they were eating, drinking, buying, selling, planting, building; 29on the day when Lot left Sodom, fire and brimstone rained from the sky to destroy them all. 30So it will be on the day the Son of Man is revealed. 31*On that day, a person who is on the housetop and whose belong-ings are in the house must not go down to get them, and likewise a person in the field must not return to what was left behind. 32Re-member the wife of Lot. 33*Whoever seeks to preserve his life will lose it, but whoever loses it will save it. 34I tell you, on that night there will be two people in one bed; one will be taken, the other left. 35*And there will be two women grinding meal together; one will be taken, the other left.[36]† 37*They said to him in reply, "Where, Lord?" He said to them, "Where the body is, there also the vultures will gather."

The Parable of the Persistent Widow.† ¹*Then he told them a parable about the necessity for them to pray always without becoming weary. He said, ²"There was a judge in a certain town who neither feared God nor respected any human being. ³And a widow in that town used to come to him and say, 'Render a just decision for me against my adversary.' ⁴For a long time the judge was unwilling, but eventually he thought, 'While it is true that I neither fear God nor respect any human being, ⁵*†because this widow keeps bothering me I shall deliver a just decision for her lest she finally come and strike me.' " ⁶The Lord said, "Pay attention to what the dishonest judge says. ⁷Will not God then secure the rights of his chosen ones who call out to him day and night? Will he be slow to answer them? ⁸I tell you, he will see to it that justice is done for them speedily. But when the Son of Man comes, will he find faith on earth?"

The Parable of the Pharisee and the Tax Collector. ⁹*He then addressed this parable to those who were convinced of their own righteousness and despised everyone else. ¹⁰"Two people went up to the temple area to pray; one was a Pharisee and the other was a tax collector. ¹¹The Pharisee took up his position and spoke this prayer to himself, 'O God, I thank you that I am not like the rest of humanity—greedy, dishonest, adulterous—or even like this tax collector. ¹²*I fast twice a week, and I pay tithes on my whole income.' ¹³*But the tax collector stood off at a distance and would not even raise his eyes to heaven but beat his breast and prayed, 'O God, be merciful to me a sinner.' ¹⁴*I tell you, the latter went home justified, not the former; for everyone who exalts himself will be humbled, and the one who humbles himself will be exalted."

Saying on Children and the Kingdom.† ¹⁵*†People were bringing even infants to him that he might touch them, and when the disciples saw this, they rebuked them. ¹⁶Jesus, however, called the children to himself and said, "Let the children come to me and do not prevent them; for the kingdom of God belongs to such as these ¹⁷*Amen, I say to you, whoever does not accept the kingdom of God like a child will not enter it."

The Rich Official. ¹⁸*An official asked him this question, "Good teacher, what must I do to inherit eternal life?" ¹⁹Jesus answered him "Why do you call me good? No one is good but God alone. ²⁰*You know the commandments, 'You shall not commit adultery; you shall not kill; you shall not steal; you shall not bear false witness; honor your father and your mother.' " 21And he replied, "All of these I have observed from my youth." 22*†When Jesus heard this he said to him, "There is still one thing left for you: sell all that you have and distribute it to the poor, and you will have a treasure in heaven. Then come, follow me." 23But when he heard this he became quite sad, for he was very rich.

On Riches and Renunciation. 24Jesus looked at him [now sad] and said, "How hard it is for those who have wealth to enter the kingdom of God! 25For it is easier for a camel to pass through the eye of a needle than for a rich person to enter the kingdom of God." 26Those who heard this said, "Then who can be saved?" 27*And he said, "What is impossible for human beings is possible for God." 28Then Peter said, "We have given up our possessions and followed you." 29*He said to them, "Amen, I say to you, there is no one who has given up house or wife or brothers or parents or children for the sake of the kingdom of God 30who will not receive [back] an overabundant return in this present age and eternal life in the age to come."

The Third Prediction of the Passion.† 31*†Then he took the Twelve aside and said to them, "Behold, we are going up to Jerusalem and everything written by the prophets about the Son of Man will be fulfilled. 32*He will be handed over to the Gentiles and he will be mocked and insulted and spat upon; 33and after they have scourged him they will kill him, but on the third day he will rise." 34*But they understood nothing of this; the word remained hidden from them and they failed to comprehend what he said.

The Healing of the Blind Beggar. 35*Now as he approached Jericho a blind man was sitting by the roadside begging, 36and hearing a crowd going by, he inquired what was happening. 37They told him, "Jesus of Nazareth is passing by." 38*†He shouted, "Jesus, Son of David, have pity on me!" 39The people walking in front rebuked him, telling him to be silent, but he kept calling out all the more, "Son of David, have pity on me!" 40Then Jesus stopped and ordered that he be brought to him; and when he came near, Jesus asked him, 41*"What do you want me to do for you?" He replied, "Lord, please let me see." 42*Jesus told him, "Have sight; your faith has saved you." 43He immediately received his sight and followed him, giving glory to God. When they saw this, all the people gave praise to God.

Zaccheaus the Tax Collector.† ¹He came to Jericho and intended to pass through the town. ²Now a man there named Zaccheaus, who was a chief tax collector and also a wealthy man, ³was seeking to see who Jesus was; but he could not see him because of the crowd, for he was short in stature. ⁴So he ran ahead and climbed a sycamore tree in order to see Jesus, who was about to pass that way. ⁵When he reached the place, Jesus looked up and said to him, "Zaccheaus, come down quickly, for today I must stay at your house." ⁶And he came down quickly and received him with joy. ⁷*When they all saw this, they began to grumble, saying, "He has gone to stay at the house of a sinner." ⁸*But Zaccheaus stood there and said to the Lord, "Behold, half of my possessions, Lord, I shall give to the poor, and if I have extorted anything from anyone I shall repay it four times over." ⁹*†And Jesus said to him, "Today salvation has come to this house because this man too is a descendant of Abraham. ¹⁰*†For the Son of Man has come to seek and to save what was lost."

The Parable of the Ten Gold Coins.† ¹¹*While they were listening to him speak, he proceeded to tell a parable because he was near Jerusalem and they thought that the kingdom of God would appear there immediately. ¹²*So he said, "A nobleman went off to a distant country to obtain the kingship for himself and then to return. ¹³†He called ten of his servants and gave them ten gold coins and told them, 'Engage in trade with these until I return.' ¹⁴His fellow citizens, however, despised him and sent a delegation after him to announce, 'We do not want this man to be our king.' ¹⁵But when he returned after obtaining the kingship, he had the servants called, to whom he had given the money, to learn what they had gained by trading. ¹⁶The first came forward and said, 'Sir, your gold coin has earned ten additional ones.' ¹⁷*He replied, 'Well done, good servant! You have been faithful in this very small matter; take charge of ten cities.' ¹⁸Then the second came and reported, 'Your gold coin, sir, has earned five more.' ¹⁹And to this servant too he said, 'You, take charge of five cities.' ²⁰Then the other servant came and said, 'Sir, here is your gold coin; I kept it stored away in a handkerchief, ²¹for I was afraid of you, because you are a demanding person; you take up what you did not lay down and you harvest what you did not plant.' ²²He said to him, 'With your own words I shall condemn you, you wicked servant. You knew I was a de manding person, taking up what I did not lay down and harvesting what I did not plant; ²³why did you not put my money in a bank? Then on my return I would have collected it with interest.' ²⁴And to those standing by he said, 'Take the gold coin from him and give it to the servant who has ten.' ²⁵But they said to him, 'Sir, he has ten gold coins.' ²⁶*'I tell you, to everyone who has, more will be given, but from the one who has not, even what he has will be taken away. ²⁷Now as for those enemies of mine who did not want me as their king, bring them here and slay them before me.' "

VI: THE TEACHING MINISTRY IN JERUSALEM†

The Entry into Jerusalem. ²⁸*After he had said this, he proceeded on his journey up to Jerusalem. ²⁹*As he drew near to Bethphage and Bethany at the place called the Mount of Olives, he sent two of his disciples. ³⁰*He said, "Go into the village opposite you, and as you enter it you will find a colt tethered on which no one has ever sat. Untie it and bring it here. ³¹And if anyone should ask you, 'Why are you untying it?' you will answer, 'The Master has need of it.' " ³²*So those who had been sent went off and found everything just as he had told them. ³³And as they were untying the colt, its owners said to them, "Why are you untying this colt?" ³⁴They answered, "The Master has need of it." ³⁵*So they brought it to Jesus, threw their cloaks over the colt, and helped Jesus to mount. ³⁶As he rode along, the people were spreading their cloaks on the road; ³⁷and now as he was approaching the slope of the Mount of Olives, the whole multitude of his disciples began to praise God aloud with joy for all the mighty deeds they had seen. ³⁸*†They proclaimed:

"Blessed is the king who comes
    in the name of the Lord.
Peace in heaven
    and glory in the highest."

³⁹†Some of the Pharisees in the crowd said to him, "Teacher, rebuke your disciples." ⁴⁰He said in reply, "I tell you, if they keep silent, the stones will cry out!"

The Lament for Jerusalem.† ⁴¹*As he drew near, he saw the city and wept over it, ⁴²*saying, "If this day you only knew what makes for peace—but now it is hidden from your eyes. ⁴³*†For the days are coming upon you when your enemies will raise a palisade against you; they will encircle you and hem you in on all sides.

⁴⁴*They will smash you to the ground and your children within you, and they will not leave one stone upon another within you because you did not recognize the time of your visitation."

The Cleansing of the Temple.† ⁴⁵*Then Jesus entered the temple area and proceeded to drive out those who were selling things, ⁴⁶*saying to them, "It is written, 'My house shall be a house of prayer, but you have made it a den of thieves.' " ⁴⁷*And every day he was teaching in the temple area. The chief priests, the scribes, and the leaders of the people, meanwhile, were seeking to put him to death, ⁴⁸but they could find no way to accomplish their purpose because all the people were hanging on his words.

The Authority of Jesus Questioned. ¹*One day as he was teaching the people in the temple area and proclaiming the good news, the chief priests and scribes, together with the elders, approached him ²*and said to him, "Tell us, by what authority are you doing these things? Or who is the one who gave you this authority?" ³He said to them in reply, "I shall ask you a question. Tell me, ⁴*was John's baptism of heavenly or of human origin?" ⁵*They discussed this among themselves, and said, "If we say, 'Of heavenly origin,' he will say, 'Why did you not believe him?' ⁶But if we say, 'Of human origin,' then all the people will stone us, for they are convinced that John was a prophet." ⁷So they answered that they did not know from where it came. ⁸Then Jesus said to them, "Neither shall I tell you by what authority I do these things."

The Parable of the Tenant Farmers.† ⁹*Then he proceeded to tell the people this parable. "[A] man planted a vineyard, leased it to tenant farmers, and then went on a journey for a long time. ¹⁰*At harvest time he sent a servant to the tenant farmers to receive some of the produce of the vineyard. But they beat the servant and sent him away empty-handed. ¹¹So he proceeded to send another servant, but him also they beat and insulted and sent away empty-handed. ¹²Then he proceeded to send a third, but this one too they wounded and threw out. ¹³*The owner of the vineyard said, 'What shall I do? I shall send my beloved son; maybe they will respect him.' ¹⁴But when the tenant farmers saw him they said to one another, 'This is the heir. Let us kill him that the inheritance may become ours.' ¹⁵†So they threw him out of the vineyard and killed him. What will the owner of the vineyard do to them? ¹⁶He will come and put those tenant farmers to death and turn over the vineyard to others." When the people heard this, they exclaimed, "Let it not be so!" ¹⁷*But he looked at them and asked, "What then does this scripture passage mean:

'The stone which the builders rejected
   has become the cornerstone'?

¹⁸Everyone who falls on that stone will be dashed to pieces; and it will crush anyone on whom it falls." ¹⁹*The scribes and chief priests sought to lay their hands on him at that very hour, but they feared the people, for they knew that he had addressed this parable to them.

Paying Taxes to the Emperor. ²⁰*†They watched him closely and sent agents pretending to be righteous who were to trap him in speech, in order to hand him over to the authority and power of the governor. ²¹*They posed this question to him, "Teacher, we know that what you say and teach is correct, and you show no partiality, but teach the way of God in accordance with the truth. ²²†Is it lawful for us to pay tribute to Caesar or not?" ²³Recognizing their craftiness he said to them, ²⁴†"Show me a denarius; whose image and name does it bear?" They replied, "Caesar's." ²⁵*So he said to them, "Then repay to Caesar what belongs to Caesar and to God what belongs to God." ²⁶They were unable to trap him by something he might say before the people, and so amazed were they at his reply that they fell silent.

The Question about the Resurrection. ²⁷*†Some Sadducees, those who deny that there is a resurrection, came forward and put this question to him, ²⁸*†saying, "Teacher, Moses wrote for us, 'If someone's brother dies leaving a wife but no child, his brother must take the wife and raise up descendants for his brother.' ²⁹Now there were seven brothers; the first married a woman but died childless. ³⁰Then the second ³¹and the third married her, and likewise all the seven died childless. ³²Finally the woman also died. ³³Now at the resurrection whose wife will that woman be? For all seven had been married to her." ³⁴Jesus said to them, "The children of this age marry and remarry; ³⁵but those who are deemed worthy to attain to the coming age and to the resurrection of the dead neither marry nor are given in marriage. ³⁶†They can no longer die, for they are like angels and they are the children of God because they are the ones who will rise. ³⁷*That the dead will rise even Moses made known in the passage about the bush, when he called 'Lord' the God of Abraham, the God of Isaac, and the God of Jacob; ³⁸*and he is not God of the dead but of the living, for to him all are alive." ³⁹Some of the scribes said in reply, "Teacher, you have answered well." ⁴⁰*And they no longer dared to ask him anything.

The Question about David's Son.† ⁴¹*Then he said to them, "How do they claim that the Messiah is the Son of David? ⁴²*For David himself in the Book of Psalms says:

'The Lord said to my lord,
  "Sit at my right hand
⁴³   till I make your enemies your footstool." '

⁴⁴Now if David calls him 'lord,' how can he be his son?"

Denunciation of the Scribes.

[45]*Then, within the hearing of all the people, he said to [his] disciples, [46]*"Be on guard against the scribes, who like to go around in long robes and love greetings in marketplaces, seats of honor in synagogues, and places of honor at banquets. [47]They devour the houses of widows and, as a pretext, recite lengthy prayers. They will receive a very severe condemnation."

Chapter 21

The Poor Widow's Contribution.† ¹*When he looked up he saw some wealthy people putting their offerings into the treasury ²and he noticed a poor widow putting in two small coins. ³He said, "I tell you truly, this poor widow put in more than all the rest; ⁴for those others have all made offerings from their surplus wealth, but she, from her poverty, has offered her whole livelihood."

The Destruction of the Temple Foretold.† ⁵*While some people were speaking about how the temple was adorned with costly stones and votive offerings, he said, ⁶*"All that you see here—the days will come when there will not be left a stone upon another stone that will not be thrown down."

The Signs of the End. ⁷*Then they asked him, "Teacher, when will this happen? And what sign will there be when all these things are about to happen?" ⁸*†He answered, "See that you not be deceived, for many will come in my name, saying, 'I am he,' and 'The time has come.' Do not follow them! ⁹When you hear of wars and insurrections, do not be terrified; for such things must happen first, but it will not immediately be the end." ¹⁰*Then he said to them, "Nation will rise against nation, and kingdom against kingdom. ¹¹There will be powerful earthquakes, famines, and plagues from place to place; and awesome sights and mighty signs will come from the sky.

The Coming Persecution. ¹²*†"Before all this happens, however, they will seize and persecute you, they will hand you over to the synagogues and to prisons, and they will have you led before kings and governors because of my name. ¹³It will lead to your giving testimony. ¹⁴Remember, you are not to prepare your defense beforehand, ¹⁵*†for I myself shall give you a wisdom in speaking that all your adversaries will be powerless to resist or refute. ¹⁶*You will even be handed over by parents, brothers, relatives, and friends, and they will put some of you to death. ¹⁷You will be hated by all because of my name, ¹⁸*but not a hair on your head will be destroyed. ¹⁹*By your perseverance you will secure your lives.

The Great Tribulation.† ²⁰*"When you see Jerusalem surrounded by armies, know that its desolation is at hand. ²¹*Then those in Judea must flee to the mountains. Let those within the city escape from it, and let those in the countryside not enter the city, ²²for these days are the time of punishment when all the scriptures are fulfilled.

²³*Woe to pregnant women and nursing mothers in those days, for a terrible calamity will come upon the earth and a wrathful judgment upon this people. ²⁴*†They will fall by the edge of the sword and be taken as captives to all the Gentiles; and Jerusalem will be trampled underfoot by the Gentiles until the times of the Gentiles are fulfilled.

The Coming of the Son of Man.
²⁵*"There will be signs in the sun, the moon, and the stars, and on earth nations will be in dismay, perplexed by the roaring of the sea and the waves. ²⁶*†People will die of fright in anticipation of what is coming upon the world, for the powers of the heavens will be shaken. ²⁷*And then they will see the Son of Man coming in a cloud with power and great glory. ²⁸*But when these signs begin to happen, stand erect and raise your heads because your redemption is at hand."

The Lesson of the Fig Tree.
²⁹*He taught them a lesson. "Consider the fig tree and all the other trees. ³⁰When their buds burst open, you see for yourselves and know that summer is now near; ³¹in the same way, when you see these things happening, know that the kingdom of God is near. ³²*Amen, I say to you, this generation will not pass away until all these things have taken place. ³³*Heaven and earth will pass away, but my words will not pass away.

Exhortation to Be Vigilant.
³⁴*"Beware that your hearts do not become drowsy from carousing and drunkenness and the anxieties of daily life, and that day catch you by surprise ³⁵like a trap. For that day will assault everyone who lives on the face of the earth. ³⁶*Be vigilant at all times and pray that you have the strength to escape the tribulations that are imminent and to stand before the Son of Man."

Ministry in Jerusalem.
³⁷*During the day, Jesus was teaching in the temple area, but at night he would leave and stay at the place called the Mount of Olives. ³⁸And all the people would get up early each morning to listen to him in the temple area.

~Chapter 22~

The Conspiracy against Jesus. 1*†Now the feast of Unleavened Bread, called the Passover, was drawing near, 2*and the chief priests and the scribes were seeking a way to put him to death, for they were afraid of the people. 3*†Then Satan entered into Judas, the one surnamed Iscariot, who was counted among the Twelve, 4and he went to the chief priests and temple guards to discuss a plan for handing him over to them. 5They were pleased and agreed to pay him money. 6He accepted their offer and sought a favorable opportunity to hand him over to them in the absence of a crowd.

Preparations for the Passover. 7*When the day of the feast of Unleavened Bread arrived, the day for sacrificing the Passover lamb, 8he sent out Peter and John, instructing them, "Go and make preparations for us to eat the Passover." 9They asked him, "Where do you want us to make the preparations?" 10†And he answered them, "When you go into the city, a man will meet you carrying a jar of water. Follow him into the house that he enters 11and say to the master of the house, 'The teacher says to you, "Where is the guest room where I may eat the Passover with my disciples?"' 12He will show you a large upper room that is furnished. Make the preparations there." 13*Then they went off and found everything exactly as he had told them, and there they prepared the Passover.

The Last Supper. 14*When the hour came, he took his place at table with the apostles. 15†He said to them, "I have eagerly desired to eat this Passover with you before I suffer, 16*for, I tell you, I shall not eat it [again] until there is fulfillment in the kingdom of God." 17†Then he took a cup, gave thanks, and said, "Take this and share it among yourselves; 18for I tell you [that] from this time on I shall not drink of the fruit of the vine until the kingdom of God comes." 19*†Then he took the bread, said the blessing, broke it, and gave it to them, saying, "This is my body, which will be given for you; do this in memory of me." 20*And likewise the cup after they had eaten, saying, "This cup is the new covenant in my blood, which will be shed for you.

The Betrayal Foretold. 21*"And yet behold, the hand of the one who is to betray me is with me on the table; 22for the Son of Man indeed goes as it has been determined; but woe to that man by whom he is betrayed." ²³And they began to debate among themselves who among them would do such a deed.

The Role of the Disciples.† ²⁴*Then an argument broke out among them about which of them should be regarded as the greatest. ²⁵*†He said to them, "The kings of the Gentiles lord it over them and those in authority over them are addressed as 'Benefactors'; ²⁶*but among you it shall not be so. Rather, let the greatest among you be as the youngest, and the leader as the servant. ²⁷For who is greater: the one seated at table or the one who serves? Is it not the one seated at table? I am among you as the one who serves. ²⁸It is you who have stood by me in my trials; ²⁹*and I confer a kingdom on you, just as my Father has conferred one on me, ³⁰*that you may eat and drink at my table in my kingdom; and you will sit on thrones judging the twelve tribes of Israel.

Peter's Denial Foretold.† ³¹*†"Simon, Simon, behold Satan has demanded to sift all of you like wheat, ³²but I have prayed that your own faith may not fail; and once you have turned back, you must strengthen your brothers." ³³*He said to him, "Lord, I am prepared to go to prison and to die with you." ³⁴*But he replied, "I tell you, Peter, before the cock crows this day, you will deny three times that you know me."

Instructions for the Time of Crisis. ³⁵*He said to them, "When I sent you forth without a money bag or a sack or sandals, were you in need of anything?" "No, nothing," they replied. ³⁶*†He said to them, "But now one who has a money bag should take it, and likewise a sack, and one who does not have a sword should sell his cloak and buy one. ³⁷*For I tell you that this scripture must be fulfilled in me, namely, 'He was counted among the wicked'; and indeed what is written about me is coming to fulfillment." ³⁸†Then they said, "Lord, look, there are two swords here." But he replied, "It is enough!"

The Agony in the Garden. ³⁹*Then going out he went, as was his custom, to the Mount of Olives, and the disciples followed him. ⁴⁰*When he arrived at the place he said to them, "Pray that you may not undergo the test." ⁴¹*After withdrawing about a stone's throw from them and kneeling, he prayed, ⁴²*saying, "Father, if you are willing, take this cup away from me; still, not my will but yours be done." [⁴³†And to strengthen him an angel from heaven appeared to him. ⁴⁴He was in such agony and he prayed so fervently that his sweat became like drops of blood falling on the ground.] ⁴⁵When he rose from prayer and returned to his disciples, he found them sleeping from grief. ⁴⁶*He said to them, "Why are you sleeping? Get up and pray that you may not undergo the test."

The Betrayal and Arrest of Jesus. ⁴⁷*While he was still speaking, a crowd approached and in front was one of the Twelve, a man named Judas. He went up to Jesus to kiss him. ⁴⁸Jesus said to him, "Judas, are you betraying the Son of Man with a kiss?" ⁴⁹*His disciples realized what was about to happen, and they asked, "Lord, shall we strike with a sword?" ⁵⁰*And one of them struck the high priest's servant and cut off his right ear. ⁵¹†But Jesus said in reply, "Stop, no more of this!" Then he touched the servant's ear and healed him. ⁵²*And Jesus said to the chief priests and temple guards and elders who had come for him, "Have you come out as against a robber, with swords and clubs? ⁵³*Day after day I was with you in the temple area, and you did not seize me; but this is your hour, the time for the power of darkness."

Peter's Denial of Jesus. ⁵⁴*After arresting him they led him away and took him into the house of the high priest; Peter was following at a distance. ⁵⁵They lit a fire in the middle of the courtyard and sat around it, and Peter sat down with them. ⁵⁶When a maid saw him seated in the light, she looked intently at him and said, "This man too was with him." ⁵⁷But he denied it saying, "Woman, I do not know him." ⁵⁸A short while later someone else saw him and said, "You too are one of them"; but Peter answered, "My friend, I am not." ⁵⁹About an hour later, still another insisted, "Assuredly, this man too was with him, for he also is a Galilean." ⁶⁰But Peter said, "My friend, I do not know what you are talking about." Just as he was saying this, the cock crowed, ⁶¹*†and the Lord turned and looked at Peter; and Peter remembered the word of the Lord, how he had said to him, "Before the cock crows today, you will deny me three times." ⁶²He went out and began to weep bitterly. ⁶³*The men who held Jesus in custody were ridiculing and beating him. ⁶⁴They blindfolded him and questioned him, saying, "Prophesy! Who is it that struck you?" ⁶⁵And they reviled him in saying many other things against him.

Jesus before the Sanhedrin.† ⁶⁶*†When day came the council of elders of the people met, both chief priests and scribes, and they brought him before their Sanhedrin. ⁶⁷*They said, "If you are the Messiah, tell us," but he replied to them, "If I tell you, you will not believe, ⁶⁸and if I question, you will not respond. ⁶⁹*But from this time on the Son of Man will be seated at the right hand of the power of God." [70]They all asked, "Are you then the Son of God?" He replied to them, "You say that I am." [71]Then they said, "What further need have we for testimony? We have heard it from his own mouth."

Jesus before Pilate.† ¹*Then the whole assembly of them arose and brought him before Pilate. ²*They brought charges against him, saying, "We found this man misleading our people; he opposes the payment of taxes to Caesar and maintains that he is the Messiah, a king." ³*Pilate asked him, "Are you the king of the Jews?" He said to him in reply, "You say so." ⁴*Pilate then addressed the chief priests and the crowds, "I find this man not guilty." ⁵But they were adamant and said, "He is inciting the people with his teaching throughout all Judea, from Galilee where he began even to here."

Jesus before Herod.† ⁶On hearing this Pilate asked if the man was a Galilean; ⁷*and upon learning that he was under Herod's jurisdiction, he sent him to Herod who was in Jerusalem at that time. ⁸*Herod was very glad to see Jesus; he had been wanting to see him for a long time, for he had heard about him and had been hoping to see him perform some sign. ⁹*He questioned him at length, but he gave him no answer. ¹⁰*The chief priests and scribes, meanwhile, stood by accusing him harshly. ¹¹*[Even] Herod and his soldiers treated him contemptuously and mocked him, and after clothing him in resplendent garb, he sent him back to Pilate. ¹²Herod and Pilate became friends that very day, even though they had been enemies formerly. ¹³Pilate then summoned the chief priests, the rulers, and the people ¹⁴*and said to them, "You brought this man to me and accused him of inciting the people to revolt. I have conducted my investigation in your presence and have not found this man guilty of the charges you have brought against him, ¹⁵nor did Herod, for he sent him back to us. So no capital crime has been committed by him. ¹⁶*Therefore I shall have him flogged and then release him."[17]†

The Sentence of Death. ¹⁸*But all together they shouted out, "Away with this man! Release Barabbas to us." ¹⁹(Now Barabbas had been imprisoned for a rebellion that had taken place in the city and for murder.) ²⁰Again Pilate addressed them, still wishing to release Jesus, ²¹but they continued their shouting, "Crucify him! Crucify him!" ²²Pilate addressed them a third time, "What evil has this man done? I found him guilty of no capital crime. Therefore I shall have him flogged and then release him." ²³With loud shouts, however, they persisted in calling for his crucifixion, and their voices prevailed. ²⁴The verdict of Pilate was that their demand should be granted. ²⁵So he released the man who had been imprisoned for rebellion and murder, for whom they asked, and he handed Jesus over to them to deal with as they wished.

The Way of the Cross.† ²⁶*As they led him away they took hold of a certain Simon, a Cyrenian, who was coming in from the country; and after laying the cross on him, they made him carry it behind Jesus. ²⁷A large crowd of people followed Jesus, including many women who mourned and lamented him. ²⁸*Jesus turned to them and said, "Daughters of Jerusalem, do not weep for me; weep instead for yourselves and for your children, ²⁹for indeed, the days are coming when people will say, 'Blessed are the barren, the wombs that never bore and the breasts that never nursed.' ³⁰*At that time people will say to the mountains, 'Fall upon us!' and to the hills, 'Cover us!' ³¹for if these things are done when the wood is green what will happen when it is dry?" ³²Now two others, both criminals, were led away with him to be executed.

The Crucifixion. ³³*When they came to the place called the Skull, they crucified him and the criminals there, one on his right, the other on his left. ³⁴*†[Then Jesus said, "Father, forgive them, they know not what they do."] They divided his garments by casting lots. ³⁵*The people stood by and watched; the rulers, meanwhile, sneered at him and said, "He saved others, let him save himself if he is the chosen one, the Messiah of God." ³⁶*Even the soldiers jeered at him. As they approached to offer him wine ³⁷they called out, "If you are King of the Jews, save yourself." ³⁸Above him there was an inscription that read, "This is the King of the Jews."

³⁹†Now one of the criminals hanging there reviled Jesus, saying, "Are you not the Messiah? Save yourself and us." ⁴⁰The other, however, rebuking him, said in reply, "Have you no fear of God, for you are subject to the same condemnation? ⁴¹*And indeed, we have been condemned justly, for the sentence we received corresponds to our crimes, but this man has done nothing criminal." ⁴²*Then he said, "Jesus, remember me when you come into your kingdom." ⁴³*He replied to him, "Amen, I say to you, today you will be with me in Paradise."

The Death of Jesus. ⁴⁴*†It was now about noon and darkness came over the whole land until three in the afternoon ⁴⁵*because of an eclipse of the sun. Then the veil of the temple was torn down the middle. ⁴⁶*Jesus cried out in a loud voice, "Father, into your hands I commend my spirit"; and when he had said this he breathed his last.

47†The centurion who witnessed what had happened glorified God and said, "This man was innocent beyond doubt." 48*When all the people who had gathered for this spectacle saw what had happened, they returned home beating their breasts; 49*but all his acquaintances stood at a distance, including the women who had followed him from Galilee and saw these events.

The Burial of Jesus. 50*Now there was a virtuous and righteous man named Joseph who, though he was a member of the council, 51*had not consented to their plan of action. He came from the Jewish town of Arimathea and was awaiting the kingdom of God. 52He went to Pilate and asked for the body of Jesus. 53*After he had taken the body down, he wrapped it in a linen cloth and laid him in a rock-hewn tomb in which no one had yet been buried. 54It was the day of preparation, and the sabbath was about to begin. 55*The women who had come from Galilee with him followed behind, and when they had seen the tomb and the way in which his body was laid in it, 56*they returned and prepared spices and perfumed oils. Then they rested on the sabbath according to the commandment.

❧ Chapter 24 ❧

The Resurrection of Jesus. [1]*But at daybreak on the first day of the week they took the spices they had prepared and went to the tomb. [2]They found the stone rolled away from the tomb; [3]but when they entered, they did not find the body of the Lord Jesus. [4]*While they were puzzling over this, behold, two men in dazzling garments appeared to them. [5]*They were terrified and bowed their faces to the ground. They said to them, "Why do you seek the living one among the dead? [6]†He is not here, but he has been raised. Remember what he said to you while he was still in Galilee, [7]*that the Son of Man must be handed over to sinners and be crucified, and rise on the third day." [8]*And they remembered his words. [9]*†Then they returned from the tomb and announced all these things to the eleven and to all the others. [10]*The women were Mary Magdalene, Joanna, and Mary the mother of James; the others who accompanied them also told this to the apostles, [11]but their story seemed like nonsense and they did not believe them. [12]*†But Peter got up and ran to the tomb, bent down, and saw the burial cloths alone; then he went home amazed at what had happened.

      The Appearance on the Road to Emmaus.† [13]*†Now that very day two of them were going to a village seven miles from Jerusalem called Emmaus, [14]and they were conversing about all the things that had occurred. [15]And it happened that while they were conversing and debating, Jesus himself drew near and walked with them, [16]*†but their eyes were prevented from recognizing him. [17]He asked them, "What are you discussing as you walk along?" They stopped, looking downcast. [18]One of them, named Cleopas, said to him in reply, "Are you the only visitor to Jerusalem who does not know of the things that have taken place there in these days?" [19]*And he replied to them, "What sort of things?" They said to him, "The things that happened to Jesus the Nazarene, who was a prophet mighty in deed and word before God and all the people, [20]how our chief priests and rulers both handed him over to a sentence of death and crucified him. [21]*But we were hoping that he would be the one to redeem Israel; and besides all this, it is now the third day since this took place. [22]*Some women from our group, however, have astounded us: they were at the tomb early in the morning ²³and did not find his body; they came back and reported that they had indeed seen a vision of angels who announced that he was alive. ²⁴*Then some of those with us went to the tomb and found things just as the women had described, but him they did not see." ²⁵*And he said to them, "Oh, how foolish you are! How slow of heart to believe all that the prophets spoke! ²⁶†Was it not necessary that the Messiah should suffer these things and enter into his glory?" ²⁷*Then beginning with Moses and all the prophets, he interpreted to them what referred to him in all the scriptures. ²⁸As they approached the village to which they were going, he gave the impression that he was going on farther. ²⁹But they urged him, "Stay with us, for it is nearly evening and the day is almost over." So he went in to stay with them. ³⁰And it happened that, while he was with them at table, he took bread, said the blessing, broke it, and gave it to them. ³¹With that their eyes were opened and they recognized him, but he vanished from their sight. ³²Then they said to each other, "Were not our hearts burning [within us] while he spoke to us on the way and opened the scriptures to us?" ³³So they set out at once and returned to Jerusalem where they found gathered together the eleven and those with them ³⁴*who were saying, "The Lord has truly been raised and has appeared to Simon!" ³⁵Then the two recounted what had taken place on the way and how he was made known to them in the breaking of the bread.

The Appearance to the Disciples in Jerusalem.† ³⁶*While they were still speaking about this, he stood in their midst and said to them, "Peace be with you." ³⁷*But they were startled and terrified and thought that they were seeing a ghost. ³⁸Then he said to them, "Why are you troubled? And why do questions arise in your hearts? ³⁹†Look at my hands and my feet, that it is I myself. Touch me and see, because a ghost does not have flesh and bones as you can see I have." ⁴⁰*And as he said this, he showed them his hands and his feet. ⁴¹While they were still incredulous for joy and were amazed, he asked them, "Have you anything here to eat?" ⁴²*They gave him a piece of baked fish; ⁴³he took it and ate it in front of them.

⁴⁴*He said to them, "These are my words that I spoke to you while I was still with you, that everything written about me in the law of Moses and in the prophets and psalms must be fulfilled." ⁴⁵*Then he opened their minds to understand the scriptures. ⁴⁶*†And he said to them, "Thus it is written that the Messiah would suffer and rise from the dead on the third day ⁴⁷*and that repentance, for the

forgiveness of sins, would be preached in his name to all the nations, beginning from Jerusalem. ⁴⁸*You are witnesses of these things. ⁴⁹*†And [behold] I am sending the promise of my Father upon you; but stay in the city until you are clothed with power from on high."

The Ascension.† ⁵⁰*Then he led them [out] as far as Bethany, raised his hands, and blessed them. ⁵¹As he blessed them he parted from them and was taken up to heaven. ⁵²*They did him homage and then returned to Jerusalem with great joy, ⁵³†and they were continually in the temple praising God.

References and Footnotes on Luke

1, 1–4:	Acts 1, 1; 1 Cor 15, 3.	48:	11, 27; 1 Sm 1, 11; 2 Sm 16, 12; 2 Kgs 14, 26; Ps 113, 7.
2:	24, 48; Jn 15, 27; Acts 1, 21–22.		
5:	1 Chr 24, 10.	49:	Dt 10, 21; Pss 71, 19; 111, 9; 126, 2–3.
7:	Gn 18, 11; Jgs 13, 2–5; 1 Sm 1, 5–6.		
9:	Ex 30, 7.	50:	Pss 89, 2; 103, 13.17.
13:	1, 57.60.63; Mt 1, 20–21.	51:	Pss 89, 10; 118, 15; Jer 32, 17 (39, 17 LXX).
15:	7, 33; Nm 6, 1–21; Jgs 13, 4; 1 Sm 1, 11 LXX.	52:	1 Sm 2, 7; 2 Sm 22, 28; Jb 5, 11; 12, 19; Ps 147, 6; Sir 10, 14; Jas 4, 6; 1 Pt 5, 5.
17:	Sir 48, 10; Mal 3, 1; 3, 23–24; Mt 11, 14; 17, 11–13.		
19:	Dn 8, 16; 9, 21.	53:	1 Sm 2, 5; Ps 107, 9.
20:	1, 45.	54:	Pss 98, 3; Is 41, 8–9.
25:	Gn 30, 23.		
27:	2, 5; Mt 1, 16.18.	55:	Gn 13, 15; 17, 7; 18, 18; 22, 17–18; Mi 7, 20.
28:	Jgs 6, 12; Ru 2, 4; Jdt 13, 18.		
31:	Gn 16, 11; Jgs 13, 3; Is 7, 14; Mt 1, 21–23.	58:	1, 14.
		59:	2, 21; Gn 17, 10.12; Lv 12, 3.
32–33:	2 Sm 7, 12.13.16; Is 9, 7.	60:	1, 13.
33:	Dn 2, 44; 7, 14; Mi 4, 7; Mt 28, 18.	64:	1, 20.
		68:	7, 16; Pss 41, 13; 72, 18; 106, 48; 111, 9.
35:	Mt 1, 20.	69:	Ps 18, 3.
37:	Gn 18, 14; Jer 32, 27; Mt 19, 26.	71:	Ps 106, 10.
		72:	Ps 106, 45–46.
		72–73:	Gn 17, 7; Lv 26, 42; Ps 105, 8–9; Mi 7, 20.
41:	1, 15; Gn 25, 22 LXX.		
42:	11, 27–28; Jgs 5, 24; Jdt 13, 18; Dt 28, 4.	73–74:	Gn 22, 16–17.
		75:	Ti 2, 12.
		76:	Is 40, 3; Mal 3, 1; Mt 3, 3; 11, 10.
45:	1, 20.		
46–55:	1 Sm 2, 1–10.		
46:	Ps 35, 9; Is 61, 10; Hb 3, 18.	78:	Mal 3, 20.
		78–79:	Is 60, 1–2.
47:	Ti 3, 4; Jude 25.	80:	2, 40; Mt 3, 1.

1, 1–4: The Gospel according to Luke is the only one of the synoptic gospels to begin with a literary prologue. Making use of a formal, literary construction and vocabulary, the author writes the prologue in imitation of Hellenistic Greek writers and, in so doing, relates his story about Jesus to contemporaneous Greek and Roman literature. Luke is not only interested in the words and deeds of Jesus, but also in the larger context of the birth, ministry, death, and resurrection of Jesus as the fulfillment of the promises of God in the Old Testament. As a second- or third-generation Christian, Luke acknowledges his debt to earlier *eyewitnesses* and *ministers of the word,* but claims that his contribution to this developing tradition is a complete and accurate account, told in an orderly manner, and intended to provide *Theophilus* ("friend of God," literally) and other readers with certainty about earlier teachings they have received.

1, 5—2, 52: Like the Gospel according to Matthew, this gospel opens with an infancy narrative, a collection of stories about the birth and childhood of Jesus. The narrative uses early Christian traditions about the birth of Jesus, traditions about the birth and circumcision of John the Baptist, and canticles such as the Magnificat (1, 46–55) and Benedictus (1, 67–79), composed of phrases drawn from the Greek Old Testament. It is largely, however, the composition of Luke who writes in imitation of Old Testament birth stories, combining historical and legendary details, literary ornamentation and interpretation of scripture, to answer in advance the question, "Who is Jesus Christ?" The focus of the narrative, therefore, is primarily christological. In this section Luke announces many of the themes that will become prominent in the rest of the gospel: the centrality of Jerusalem and the temple, the journey motif, the universality of salvation, joy and peace, concern for the lowly, the importance of women, the presentation of Jesus as savior, Spirit-guided revelation and prophecy, and the fulfillment of Old Testament promises. The account presents parallel scenes (diptychs) of angelic announcements of the birth of John the Baptist and of Jesus, and of the birth, circumcision, and presentation of John and Jesus. In this parallelism, the ascendency of Jesus over John is stressed: John is prophet of the Most High (1, 76); Jesus is Son of the Most High (1, 32). John is great in the sight of the Lord (1, 15); Jesus will be Great (a LXX attribute, used absolutely, of God) (1, 32). John will go before the Lord (1, 16–17); Jesus will be Lord (1, 43; 2, 11).

1, 5: *In the days of Herod, King of Judea:* Luke relates the story of salvation history to events in contemporary world history. Here and in 3, 1–2, he connects his narrative with events in Palestinian history; in 2, 1–2 and 3, 1, he casts the Jesus story in the light of events of Roman history. Herod the Great, the son of the Idumean Antipater, was declared "King of Judea" by the Roman Senate in 40 B.C., but became the undisputed ruler of Palestine only in 37 B.C. He continued as king until his death in 4 B.C. *Priestly division of Abijah:* a reference to the eighth of the twenty-four divisions of priests who, for a week at a time, twice a year, served in the Jerusalem temple.

1, 7: *They had no child:* though childlessness was looked upon in contemporaneous Judaism as a curse or punishment for sin, it is intended here to present Elizabeth in a situation similar to that of some of the great mothers of important Old Testament figures: Sarah (Gn 15, 3; 16, 1); Rebekah (Gn 25, 21); Rachel (Gn 29, 31; 30, 1); the mother of Samson and wife of Manoah (Jgs 13, 2–3); Hannah (1 Sm 1, 2).

1, 13: *Do not be afraid:* a stereotyped Old Testament phrase spoken to reassure the recipient of a heavenly vision (Gn 15, 1; Jos 1, 9; Dn 10, 12.19 and elsewhere in 1, 30; 2, 10). *You shall name him John:* the name means "Yahweh has shown favor," an indication of John's role in salvation history.

1, 15: *He will drink neither wine nor strong drink:* like Samson (Jgs 13, 4–5) and Samuel (1 Sm 1, 11 LXX and 4QSamᵃ), John is to be consecrated by Nazirite vow and set apart for the Lord's service.

1, 17: *He will go before him in the spirit and power of Elijah:* John is to be the messenger sent before Yahweh, as described in Mal 3, 1–2. He is cast, moreover, in the role of the Old Testament fiery reformer, the prophet Elijah, who according to Mal 3, 23 (4, 5) is sent before "the great and terrible day of the Lord comes."

1, 19: *I am Gabriel:* "the angel of the Lord" is identified as Gabriel, the angel who in Dn 9, 20–25 announces the seventy weeks of years and the coming of an anointed one, a prince. By alluding to Old Testament themes in vv 17 and 19, such as the coming of the day of the Lord and the dawning of the messianic era, Luke is presenting his interpretation of the significance of the births of John and Jesus.

1, 20: *You will be speechless and unable to talk:*

Zechariah's becoming mute is the sign given in response to his question in v 18. When Mary asks a similar question in 1, 34, unlike Zechariah who was punished for his doubt, she, in spite of her doubt, is praised and reassured (35–37).

1, 26–38: The announcement to Mary of the birth of Jesus is parallel to the announcement to Zechariah of the birth of John. In both the angel Gabriel appears to the parent who is troubled by the vision (11–12.26–29) and then told by the angel not to fear (13.30). After the announcement is made (14–17.31–33) the parent objects (18.34) and a sign is given to confirm the announcement (20.36). The particular focus of the announcement of the birth of Jesus is on his identity as Son of David (32–33) and Son of God (32.35).

1, 32: *Son of the Most High:* cf 1, 76 where John is described as "prophet of the Most High." "Most High" is a title for God commonly used by Luke (35.76; 6, 35; 8, 28; Acts 7, 48; 16, 17).

1, 34: Mary's questioning response is a denial of sexual relations and is used by Luke to lead to the angel's declaration about the Spirit's role in the conception of this child (35). According to Luke, the virginal conception of Jesus takes place through the holy Spirit, the power of God, and therefore Jesus has a unique relationship to Yahweh: he is Son of God.

1, 36–37: The sign given to Mary in confirmation of the angel's announcement to her is the pregnancy of her aged relative Elizabeth. If a woman past the childbearing age could become pregnant, why, the angel implies, should there be doubt about Mary's pregnancy, for *nothing will be impossible for God.*

1, 43: Even before his birth, Jesus is identified in Lk as the *Lord.*

1, 45: *Blessed are you who believed:* Luke portrays Mary as a believer whose faith stands in contrast to the disbelief of Zechariah (20). Mary's role as believer in the infancy narrative should be seen in connection with the explicit mention of her presence among "those who believed" after the resurrection at the beginning of the Acts of the Apostles (14).

1, 46–55: Although Mary is praised for being the mother of the Lord and because of her belief, she reacts as the servant in a psalm of praise, the Magnificat. Because there is no specific connection of the canticle to the context of Mary's pregnancy and her visit to Elizabeth, the Magnificat (with the possible exception of v 48) may have been a Jewish Christian hymn that Luke found appropriate at this point in his story. Even if not composed by Luke, it fits in well with themes found elsewhere in Lk: joy and exultation in the Lord; the lowly being singled out for God's favor; the reversal of human fortunes; the fulfillment of Old Testament promises. The loose connection between the hymn and the context is further seen in the fact that a few Old Latin manuscripts identify the speaker of the hymn as Elizabeth, even though the overwhelming textual evidence makes Mary the speaker.

1, 57–66: The birth and circumcision of John above all emphasize John's incorporation into the people of Israel by the sign of the covenant (Gn 17, 1–12). The narrative of John's circumcision also prepares the way for the subsequent description of the circumcision of Jesus in 2, 21. At the beginning of his two-volume work Luke shows those who play crucial roles in the inauguration of Christianity to be wholly a part of the people of Israel. At the end of the Acts of the Apostles (21, 20; 22, 3; 23, 6–9; 24, 14–16; 26, 2–8.22–23) he will argue that Christianity is the direct descendant of Pharisaic Judaism.

1, 59: The practice of Palestinian Judaism at this time was to name the child at birth; moreover, though naming a male child after the father is not completely unknown, the usual practice was to name the child after the grandfather (see 61). The naming of the child John

and Zechariah's recovery from his loss of speech should be understood as fulfilling the angel's announcement to Zechariah in 1, 13 and 20.

1, 68–79: Like the canticle of Mary (46–55) the canticle of Zechariah is only loosely connected with its context. Apart from vv 76–77, the hymn in speaking of *a horn for our salvation* (69) and *the daybreak from on high* (78) applies more closely to Jesus and his work than to John. Again like Mary's canticle, it is largely composed of phrases taken from the Greek Old Testament and may have been a Jewish Christian hymn of praise that Luke adapted to fit the present context by inserting vv 76–77 to give Zechariah's reply to the question asked in v 66.

1, 69: *A horn for our salvation:* the horn is a common Old Testament figure for strength (Pss 18, 3; 75, 5–6; 89, 18; 112, 9; 148, 14). This description is applied to God in Ps 18, 3 and is here transferred to Jesus. The connection of the phrase with *the house of David* gives the title messianic overtones and may indicate an allusion to a phrase in Hannah's song of praise (1 Sm 2, 10), "the horn of his anointed."

1, 76: *You will go before the Lord:* here *the Lord* is most likely a reference to Jesus (contrast 15–17 where Yahweh is meant) and John is presented as the precursor of Jesus.

1, 78: *The daybreak from on high:* three times in the LXX (Jer 23, 5; Zec 3, 8; 6, 12), the Greek word used here for *daybreak* translates the Hebrew word for "scion, branch," an Old Testament messianic title.

*Chapter Two References

2, 4: Mi 5, 2; Mt 2, 6.	34: 12, 51; Is 8, 14;
5: 1, 27; Mt 1, 18.	Jn 9, 39; Rom 9,
7: Mt 1, 25.	33; 1 Cor 1, 23;
9: 1, 11.26.	1 Pt 2, 7–8.
11: Mt 1, 21; 16, 16;	38: Is 52, 9.
Jn 4, 42; Acts 2,	39: Mt 2, 23.
36; 5, 31; Phil 2,	40: 1, 80; 2, 52.
11.	41: Ex 12, 24–27;
14: 19, 38.	23, 15; Dt 16,
21: 1, 31; Gn 17, 12;	1–8.
Mt 1, 21.	51: 2, 19.
22–24: Lv 12, 2–8.	52: 1, 80; 2, 40;
23: Ex 13, 2.12.	1 Sm 2, 26.
30–31: 3, 6; Is 40, 5	
LXX; 52, 10.	
32: Is 42, 6; 46, 13;	
49, 6; Acts 13,	
47; 26, 23.	

†Chapter Two Footnotes

2, 1–2: Although universal registrations of Roman citizens are attested in 28 B.C., 8 B.C., and A.D. 14 and enrollments in individual provinces of those who are not Roman citizens are also attested, such a universal census of the Roman world under Caesar Augustus is unknown outside the New Testament. Moreover, there are notorious historical problems connected with Luke's dating the census *when Quirinius was governor of Syria,* and the various attempts to resolve the difficulties have proved unsuccessful. P. Sulpicius Quirinius became legate of the province of Syria in A.D. 6–7 when Judea was annexed to the province of Syria. At that time, a provincial census of Judea was taken up. If Quirinius had been legate of Syria previously, it would have to have been before 10 B.C. because the various legates of Syria from 10 B.C. to 4 B.C. (the death of Herod) are known, and such a dating for an earlier census under Quirinius would create additional problems for dating the beginning of Jesus' ministry (3, 1.23). A previous legateship after 4 B.C. (and before A.D. 6) would not fit with the dating of Jesus' birth in the days of Herod (1, 5; Mt 2, 1). Luke may simply be combining Jesus' birth in Bethlehem with his vague recollection of a census under Quirinius (see also Acts 5, 37) to underline the significance of this birth for the whole Roman world: through this child born in Bethlehem peace and salvation come to the empire.

2, 1: *Caesar Augustus:* the reign of the Roman emperor Caesar Augustus is usually dated from 27 B.C. to his death in A.D. 14. According to Greek inscriptions, Augustus was regarded in the Roman Empire as "savior" and "god," and he was credited with establishing a time of peace, the *pax Augusta,* throughout the Roman world during his long reign. It is not by chance that Luke relates the birth of Jesus to the time of Caesar Augustus: the real savior (11) and peace-bearer (14; see also 19, 38) is the child born in Bethlehem. The great emperor is simply God's agent (like the Persian king Cyrus in Is 44, 28—45, 1) who provides the occasion for God's purposes to be accomplished. *The whole world:* that is, the whole Roman world: Rome, Italy, and the Roman provinces.

2, 7: *Firstborn son:* the description of Jesus as *firstborn son* does not necessarily mean that Mary had other sons. It is a legal description indicating that Jesus possessed the rights and privileges of the firstborn son (Gn 27; Ex 13, 2; Nm 3, 12–13; 18, 15–16; Dt 21, 15–17). See the notes on Mt 1, 25 and Mk 6, 3. *Wrapped him in swaddling clothes:* there may be an allusion here to the birth of another descendant of David, his son Solomon, who though a great king was wrapped in swaddling clothes like any other infant (Wis 7, 4–6). *Laid him in a manger:* a feeding trough for animals. A possible allusion to Is 1, 3 LXX.

2, 8–20: The announcement of Jesus' birth to the shepherds is in keeping with Luke's theme that the lowly are singled out as the recipients of God's favors and blessings (see also 1, 48.52).

2, 11: The basic message of the infancy narrative is contained in the angel's announcement: this child is *savior, Messiah,* and *Lord.* Luke is the only synoptic gospel writer to use the title *savior* for Jesus (11; Acts 5, 31; 13, 23; see also 1, 69; 19, 9; Acts 4, 12). As savior, Jesus is looked upon by Luke as the one who rescues humanity from sin and delivers humanity from the condition of alienation from God. The title *christos,* "Christ," is the Greek equivalent of the Hebrew *māšîaḥ,* "Messiah," "anointed one." Among certain groups in first-century Palestinian Judaism, the title was applied to an expected royal leader from the line of David who would restore the kingdom to Israel (see Acts 1, 6). The political overtones of the title are played down in Lk and instead the Messiah of the Lord (26) or the Lord's anointed is the one who now brings salvation to all humanity, Jew and Gentile (29–32). *Lord* is the most frequently used title for Jesus in Lk and Acts. In the New Testament it is also applied to Yahweh, as it is in the Old Testament. When used of Jesus it points to his transcendence and dominion over humanity.

2, 14: *On earth peace to those on whom his favor rests:* the peace that results from the Christ event is for those whom God has favored with his grace. This reading is found in the oldest representatives of the Western and Alexandrian text traditions and is the preferred one; the Byzantine text tradition, on the other hand, reads: "on earth peace, good will toward men." The peace of which Luke's gospel speaks (14; 7, 50; 8, 48; 10, 5–6; 19, 38.42; 24, 36) is more than the absence of war or the *pax Augusta;* it also includes the security and well-being characteristic of peace in the Old Testament.

2, 21: Just as John before him had been incorporated into the people of Israel through his circumcision, so too this child (see the note on 1, 57–66).

2, 22–40: The presentation of Jesus in the temple depicts the parents of Jesus as devout Jews, faithful observers of the law of the Lord (23.24.39), i.e., the law of Moses. In this respect, they are described in a fashion similar to the parents of John (1, 6) and Simeon (25) and Anna (36–37).

2, 22: *Their purification:* syntactically, *their* must refer to Mary and Joseph, even though the Mosaic law never mentions the purification of the husband. Recognizing the problem, some Western scribes have altered the text to read "his purification," understanding the presentation of Jesus in the temple as a form of purification; the Vulgate version has a Latin form that could be either "his" or "her." According to the Mosaic law (Lv 12, 2–8), the woman who gives birth to a boy is unable for forty days to touch anything sacred or to enter the temple area by reason of her legal impurity. At the end of this period she is required to offer a year-old lamb as a burnt offering and a turtledove or young pigeon as an expiation of sin. The woman who could not afford a lamb offered instead two turtledoves or two young pigeons, as Mary does here. *They took him up to Jerusalem to present him to the Lord:* as the firstborn son (7) Jesus was consecrated to the Lord as the law required (Ex 13, 2.12), but there was no requirement that this be done at the temple. The concept of a presentation at the temple is probably derived from 1 Sm 1, 24–28, where Hannah offers the child Samuel for sanctuary services. The law further stipulated (Nm 3, 47–48) that the firstborn son should be redeemed by the parents through their payment of five shekels to a member of a priestly family. About this legal requirement Luke is silent.

2, 25: *Awaiting the consolation of Israel:* Simeon here and later Anna who speak about the child to all who were awaiting the redemption of Jerusalem represent the hopes and expectations of faithful and devout Jews who at this time were looking forward to the restoration of God's rule in Israel. The birth of Jesus brings these hopes to fulfillment.

2, 35: *(And you yourself a sword will pierce):* Mary herself will not be untouched by the various reactions to the role of Jesus (34). Her blessedness as mother of the Lord will be challenged by her son who describes true blessedness as "hearing the word of God and observing it" (11, 27–28 and 8, 20–21).

2, 41–52: This story's concern with an incident from Jesus' youth is unique in the canonical gospel tradition. It presents Jesus in the role of the faithful Jewish boy, raised in the traditions of Israel, and fulfilling all that the law requires. With this episode, the infancy narrative ends just as it began, in the setting of the Jerusalem temple.

2, 49: *I must be in my Father's house:* this phrase can also be translated, "I must be about my Father's work." In either translation, Jesus refers to God as his Father. His divine sonship, and his obedience to his heavenly Father's will, take precedence over his ties to his family.

*Chapter Three References

3, 1–20: Mt 3, 1–12; Mk 1, 1–8; Jn 1, 19–28.
2: 1, 80.
3: Acts 13, 24; 19, 4.
4–6: Is 40, 3–5.
4: Jn 1, 23.
6: 2, 30–31.
7: Mt 12, 34.
8: Jn 8, 39.
9: Mt 7, 19; Jn 15, 6.
12: 7, 29.
15–16: Acts 13, 25.
16: 7, 19–20; Jn 1, 27; Acts 1, 5; 11, 16.
17: Mt 3, 12.
19–20: Mt 14, 3–4; Mk 6, 17–18.
21–22: Mt 3, 13–17; Mk 1, 9–11.

22: 9, 35; Ps 2, 7; Is 42, 1; Mt 12, 18; 17, 5; Mk 9, 7; Jn 1, 32; 2 Pt 1, 17.
23–38: Mt 1, 1–17.
23: 4, 22; Jn 6, 42.
27: 1 Chr 3, 17; Ez 3, 2.
31: 2 Sm 5, 14.
31–32: 1 Sm 16, 1.18.
31–33: Ru 4, 17–22; 1 Chr 2, 1–15.
33: Gn 29, 35; 38, 29.
34: Gn 21, 3; 25, 26; 1 Chr 1, 34; 28, 34.
34–36: Gn 11, 10–26; 1 Chr 1, 24–27.
36–38: Gn 4, 25—5, 32; 1 Chr 1, 1–4.

†Chapter Three Footnotes

3, 1–20: Although Luke is indebted in this section to his sources, the Gospel of Mark and a collection of sayings of John the Baptist, he has clearly marked this introduction to the ministry of Jesus with his own individual style. Just as the gospel began with a long periodic sentence (1, 1–4), so too this section (1–2) he casts the call of John the Baptist in the form of an Old Testament prophetic call (2) and extends the quotation from Isaiah found in Mk 1, 3 (Is 40, 3) by the addition of Is 40, 4–5 in vv 5–6. In doing so, he presents his theme of the universality of salvation, which he has announced earlier in the words of Simeon (2, 30–32). Moreover, in describing the expectation of the people (15), Luke is characterizing the time of John's preaching in the same way as he had earlier described the situation of other devout Israelites in the infancy narrative (2, 25–26.37–38). In vv 7–18 Luke presents the preaching of John the Baptist who urges the crowds to reform in view of *the coming wrath* (7.9: eschatological preaching), and who offers the crowds certain standards for reforming social conduct (10–14: ethical preaching), and who announces to the crowds the coming of *one mightier than* he (15–18: messianic preaching).

3, 1: *Tiberius Caesar:* Tiberius succeeded Augustus as emperor in A.D. 14 and reigned until A.D. 37. The fifteenth year of his reign, depending on the method of calculating his first regnal year, would have fallen between A.D. 27 and 29. *Pontius Pilate:* prefect of Judea from A.D. 26 to 36. The Jewish historian Josephus describes him as a greedy and ruthless prefect who had little regard for the local Jewish population and their religious practices (see 13, 1). *Herod:* i.e., Herod Antipas, the son of Herod the Great. He ruled over Galilee and Perea from 4 B.C. to A.D. 39. His official title *tetrarch* means literally, "ruler of a quarter," but came to designate any subordinate prince. *Philip:* also a son of Herod the Great, tetrarch of the territory to the north and east of the Sea of Galilee from 4 B.C. to A.D. 34. Only two small areas of this territory are mentioned by Luke. *Lysanias:* nothing is known about this Lysanias who is said here to have been tetrarch of Abilene, a territory northwest of Damascus.

3, 2: *During the high priesthood of Annas and Caiaphas:* after situating the call of John the Baptist in terms of the civil rulers of the period, Luke now mentions the religious leadership of Palestine (see the note on 1, 5). Annas had been high priest A.D. 6–15. After be-

ing deposed by the Romans in A.D. 15 he was succeeded by various members of his family and eventually by his son-in-law, Caiaphas, who was high priest A.D. 18–36. Luke refers to Annas as high priest at this time (but see Jn 18, 13.19), possibly because of the continuing influence of Annas or because the title continued to be used for the ex-high priest. *The word of God came to John:* Luke is alone among the New Testament writers in associating the preaching of John with a call from God. Luke is thereby identifying John with the prophets whose ministries began with similar calls. In 7, 26 John will be described as "more than a prophet"; he is also the precursor of Jesus (7, 27), a transitional figure inaugurating the period of the fulfillment of prophecy and promise.

3, 3: See the note on Mt 3, 2.

3, 4: The Essenes from Qumran used the same passage to explain why their community was in the desert studying and observing the law and the prophets (1QS 8, 12–15).

3, 16: *He will baptize you with the holy Spirit and fire:* in contrast to John's baptism with water, Jesus is said to baptize with the holy Spirit and with fire. From the point of view of the early Christian community, the Spirit and fire must have been understood in the light of the fire symbolism of the pouring out of the Spirit at Pentecost (Acts 2, 1–4); but as part of John's preaching, the Spirit and fire should be related to their purifying and refining characteristics (Ez 36, 25–27; Mal 3, 2–3). See the note on Mt 3, 11.

3, 17: *Winnowing fan:* see the note on Mt 3, 12.

3, 19–20: Luke separates the ministry of John the Baptist from that of Jesus by reporting the imprisonment of John before the baptism of Jesus (21–22). Luke uses this literary device to serve his understanding of the periods of salvation history. With John the Baptist, the time of promise, the period of Israel, comes to an end; with the baptism of Jesus and the descent of the Spirit upon him, the time of fulfillment, the period of Jesus, begins. In his second volume, the Acts of the Apostles, Luke will introduce the third epoch in salvation history, the period of the church.

3, 21–22: This episode in Luke focuses on the heavenly message identifying Jesus as *Son* and, through the allusion to Is 42, 1, as Servant of Yahweh. The relationship of Jesus to the Father has already been announced in the infancy narrative (1, 32.35; 2, 49); it occurs here at the beginning of Jesus' Galilean ministry and will reappear in 9, 35 before another major section of Luke's gospel, the travel narrative (9, 51—19, 27). Elsewhere in Luke's writings (4, 18; Acts 10, 38), this incident will be interpreted as a type of anointing of Jesus.

3, 21: *Was praying:* Luke regularly presents Jesus at prayer at important points in his ministry: here at his baptism; at the choice of the Twelve (6, 12); before Peter's confession (9, 18); at the transfiguration (9, 28); when he teaches his disciples to pray (11, 1); at the Last Supper (22, 32); on the Mount of Olives (22, 41); on the cross (23, 46).

3, 22: *You are my beloved Son; with you I am well pleased:* this is the best attested reading in the Greek manuscripts. The Western reading, "You are my Son, this day I have begotten you," is derived from Ps 2, 7.

3, 23–38: Whereas Mt 1, 2 begins the genealogy of Jesus with Abraham to emphasize Jesus' bonds with the people of Israel, Luke's universalism leads him to trace the descent of Jesus beyond Israel to Adam and beyond that to God (38) to stress again Jesus' divine sonship.

3, 31: *The son of Nathan, the son of David:* in keeping with Jesus' prophetic role in Lk and Acts (e.g., 7, 16.39; 9, 8; 13, 33; 24, 19; Acts 3, 22–23; 7, 37) Luke traces Jesus' Davidic ancestry through the prophet Nathan (see 2 Sm 7, 2) rather than through King Solomon, as Mt 1, 6–7.

*Chapter Four References

4, 1–13: Mt 4, 1–11; Mk
1, 12–13.
2: Heb 4, 15.
4: Dt 8, 3.
6: Jer 27, 5; Mt 28,
18.
8: Dt 6, 13.
10: Ps 91, 11.
11: Ps 91, 12.
12: Dt 6, 16; 1 Cor
10, 9.
13: 22, 3; Jn 13,
2.27; Heb 4, 15.
14–15: Mt 4, 12–17; Mk
1, 14–15.
14: 5, 15; Mt 3, 16.
16–30: Mt 13, 53–58;
Mk 6, 1–6.
18–19: Is 61, 1–2; 58, 6.
22: 3, 23; Jn 6, 42.
25: 1 Kgs 17, 1–7;
18, 1; Jas 5, 17.

26: 1 Kgs 17, 9.
27: 2 Kgs 5, 1–14.
31–37: Mk 1, 21–28.
31: Mt 4, 13; Jn 2,
12.
32: Mt 7, 28–29.
33–34: 8, 28; Mt 8, 29;
Mk 1, 23–24; 5,
7.
34: 4, 41; Jn 6, 69.
38–39: Mt 8, 14–15; Mk
1, 29–31.
40–41: Mt 8, 16; Mk 1,
32–34.
41: 4, 34; Mt 8, 29;
Mk 3, 11–12.
42–44: Mk 1, 35–39.
43: 8, 1; Mk 1,
14–15.

†Chapter Four Footnotes

4, 1–13: See the note on Mt 4, 1–11.

4, 1: *Filled with the holy Spirit:* as a result of the descent of the Spirit upon him at his baptism (3, 21–22), Jesus is now equipped to overcome the devil. Just as the Spirit is prominent at this early stage of Jesus' ministry (1.14.18), so too it will be at the beginning of the period of the church in Acts (Acts 1, 4; 2, 4.17).

4, 2: *For forty days:* the mention of forty days recalls the forty years of the wilderness wanderings of the Israelites during the Exodus (Dt 8, 2).

4, 9: *To Jerusalem:* the Lucan order of the temptations concludes on the parapet of the temple in Jerusalem, the city of destiny in Luke-Acts. It is in Jerusalem that Jesus will ultimately face his destiny (9, 51; 13, 33).

4, 13: *For a time:* the devil's opportune time will occur before the passion and death of Jesus (Lk 22, 3.31–32.53).

4, 14: *News of him spread:* a Lucan theme; see v 37; 5, 15; 7, 17.

4, 16–30: Luke has transposed to the beginning of Jesus' ministry an incident from his Marcan source, which situated it near the end of the Galilean ministry (Mk 6, 1–6a). In doing so, Luke turns the initial admiration (22) and subsequent rejection of Jesus (28–29) into a foreshadowing of the whole future ministry of Jesus. Moreover, the rejection of Jesus in his own hometown hints at the greater rejection of him by Israel (Acts 13, 46).

4, 16: *According to his custom:* Jesus' practice of regularly attending synagogue is carried on by the early Christians' practice of meeting in the temple (Acts 2, 46; 3, 1; 5, 12).

4, 18: *The Spirit of the Lord is upon me, because he has anointed me:* see the note on 3, 21–22. As this incident develops, Jesus is portrayed as a prophet whose ministry is compared to that of the prophets Elijah and Elisha. Prophetic anointings are known in first-century Palestinian Judaism from the Qumran literature that speaks of prophets as God's anointed ones. *To bring glad tidings to the poor:* more than any other gospel writer Luke is concerned with Jesus' attitude toward the economically and socially poor (see 6, 20.24; 12, 16–21; 14, 12–14; 16, 19–26; 19, 8). At times, the poor in Luke's gospel are associated with the downtrodden, the oppressed and afflicted, the forgotten and the neglected (18; 6, 20–22; 7, 22; 14, 12–14), and it is they who accept Jesus' message of salvation.

4, 21: *Today this scripture passage is fulfilled in your hearing:* this sermon inaugurates the time of fulfillment of Old Testament prophecy. Luke presents the ministry of Jesus as fulfilling Old Testament hopes and expectations (7, 22); for Luke, even Jesus' suffering, death, and resurrection are done in fulfillment of the scriptures (24, 25–27.44–46; Acts 3, 18).

4, 23: *The things that we heard were done in Capernaum:* Luke's source for this incident reveals an awareness of an earlier ministry of Jesus in Capernaum that Luke has not yet made use of because of his transposition of this Nazareth episode to the beginning of Jesus' Galilean ministry. It is possible that by use of the future tense *you will quote me. . . ,* Jesus is being portrayed as a prophet.

4, 25–26: The references to Elijah and Elisha serve several purposes in this episode: they emphasize Luke's portrait of Jesus as a prophet like Elijah and Elisha; they help to explain why the initial admiration of the people turns to rejection; and they provide the scriptural justification for the future Christian mission to the Gentiles.

4, 26: *A widow in Zarephath in the land of Sidon:* like Naaman the Syrian in v 27, a non-Israelite becomes the object of the prophet's ministry.

4, 31–44: The next several incidents in Jesus' ministry take place in Capernaum and are based on Luke's source, Mk 1, 21–39. To the previous portrait of Jesus as prophet (16–30) they now add a presentation of him as teacher (31–32), exorcist (32–37.41), healer (38–40), and proclaimer of God's kingdom (43).

4, 34: *What have you to do with us?:* see the note on Jn 2, 4. *Have you come to destroy us?:* the question reflects the current belief that before the day of the Lord control over humanity would be wrested from the evil spirits, evil destroyed, and God's authority over humanity reestablished. The synoptic gospel tradition presents Jesus carrying out this task.

4, 38: *The house of Simon:* because of Luke's arrangement of material, the reader has not yet been introduced to Simon (cf Mk 1, 16–18.29–31). Situated as it is before the call of Simon (5, 1–11), it helps the reader to understand Simon's eagerness to do what Jesus says (5, 5) and to follow him (5, 11).

4, 41: *They knew that he was the Messiah:* that is, the Christ (see the note on 2, 11).

4, 42: *They tried to prevent him from leaving them:* the reaction of these strangers in Capernaum is presented in contrast to the reactions of those in his hometown who rejected him (28–30).

4, 44: *In the synagogues of Judea:* instead of *Judea,* which is the best reading of the manuscript tradition, the Byzantine text tradition and other manuscripts read "Galilee," a reading that harmonizes Lk with Mt 4, 23 and Mk 1, 39. Up to this point Luke has spoken only of a ministry of Jesus in Galilee. Luke may be using *Judea* to refer to the land of Israel, the territory of the Jews, and not to a specific portion of it.

*Chapter Five References

5, 1–11: Mt 4, 18–22; Mk
1, 16–20.
1–3: Mt 13, 1–2; Mk
2, 13; 3, 9–10; 4,
1–2.
4–9: Jn 21, 1–11.
10: Jer 16, 16.
11: Mt 19, 27.
12–16: Mt 8, 2–4; Mk 1,
40–45.
14: 8, 56; Lv 14,
2–32; Mk 7, 36.

16: Mk 1, 35.
17–26: Mt 9, 1–8; Mk 2,
1–12.
21: 7, 49; Is 43, 25.
22: 6, 8; 9, 47.
24–25: Jn 5, 8–9.27.
27–32: Mt 9, 9–13; Mk
2, 13–17.
29–30: 15, 1.
33–39: Mt 9, 14–17; Mk
2, 18–22.

†Chapter Five Footnotes

5, 1–11: This incident has been transposed from his source, Mk 1, 16–20, which places it immediately after Jesus makes his appearance in Galilee. By this transposition Luke uses this example of Simon's acceptance of Jesus to counter the earlier rejection of him by his home-town people, and since several incidents dealing with Jesus' power and authority have already been narrated, Luke creates a plausible context for the acceptance of Jesus by Simon and his partners. Many commentators have noted the similarity between the wondrous catch of fish reported here (4–9) and the post-resurrectional appearance of Jesus in Jn 21, 1–11. There are traces in Luke's story that the post-resurrectional context is the original one: in v 8 Simon addresses Jesus as *Lord* (a post-resurrectional title for Jesus—see 24, 34; Acts 2, 36—that has been read back into the historical ministry of Jesus) and recognizes himself as a sinner (an appropriate recognition for one who has denied knowing Jesus—22, 54–62). As used by Luke, the incident looks forward to Peter's leadership in Luke-Acts (6, 14; 9, 20; 22, 31–32; 24, 34; Acts 1, 15; 2, 14–40; 10, 11–18; 15, 7–12) and symbolizes the future success of Peter as fisherman (Acts 2, 41).

5, 11: *They left everything:* in Mk 1, 16–20 and Mt 4, 18–22 the fishermen who follow Jesus leave their nets and their father; in Luke, they leave *everything* (see also 28; 12, 33; 14, 33; 18, 22), an indication of Luke's theme of complete detachment from material possessions.

5, 12: *Full of leprosy:* see the note on Mk 1, 40.

5, 14: *Show yourself to the priest . . . what Moses prescribed:* this is a reference to Lv 14, 2–9 that gives detailed instructions for the purification of one who had been a victim of leprosy and thereby excluded from contact with others (see Lv 13, 45–46.49; Nm 5, 2–3). *That will be proof for them:* see the note on Mt 8, 4.

5, 17—6, 11: From his Marcan source, Luke now introduces a series of controversies with Pharisees: controversy over Jesus' power to forgive sins (17–26); controversy over his eating and drinking with tax collectors and sinners (27–32); controversy over not fasting (33–36); and finally two episodes narrating controversies over observance of the sabbath (1–11).

5, 17: *Pharisees:* see the note on Mt 3, 7.

5, 19: *Through the tiles:* Luke has adapted the story found in Mk to his non-Palestinian audience by changing "opened up the roof" (Mk 2, 4, a reference to Palestinian straw and clay roofs) to *through the tiles,* a detail that reflects the Hellenistic Greco-Roman house with tiled roof.

5, 20: *As for you, your sins are forgiven:* literally, "O man, your sins are forgiven you." The connection between the forgiveness of sins and the cure of the paralytic reflects the belief of first-century Palestine (based on the Old Testament: Ex 20, 5; Dt 5, 9) that sickness and infirmity are the result of sin, one's own or that of one's ancestors (see also 13, 2; Jn 5, 14; 9, 2).

5, 21: *The scribes:* see the note on Mk 2, 6.

5, 24: See the note on Mt 9, 6 and Mk 2, 10.

5, 28: *Leaving everything behind:* see the note on 5, 11.

5, 34–35: See the notes on Mt 9, 15 and Mk 2, 19.

5, 34: *Wedding guests:* literally, "sons of the bridal chamber."

5, 36–39: See the notes on Mt 9, 16–17 and Mk 2, 19.

5, 39: *The old is good:* this saying is meant to be ironic and offers an explanation for the rejection by some of the new wine that Jesus offers: satisfaction with old forms will prevent one from sampling the new.

*Chapter Six References

6, 1–5: Mt 12, 1–8; Mk 2, 23–28.
1: Dt 23, 26.
3–4: 1 Sm 21, 1–6.
4: Lv 24, 5–9.
6–11: Mt 12, 9–14; Mk 3, 1–6.
7: 14, 1.
8: 5, 22; 9, 47.
12–16: Mt 10, 1–4; Mk 3, 13–19.
14–16: Acts 1, 13.
17–19: Mt 4, 23–25; Mk 3, 7–10.
20–26: Mt 5, 1–12.
21: Ps 126, 5–6; Is 61, 3; Jer 31, 25; Rv 7, 16–17.
22: Jn 15, 19; 16, 2; 1 Pt 4, 14.
23: 11, 47–48; 2 Chr 36, 16; Mt 23, 30–31.
24: Jas 5, 1.
25: Is 65, 13–14.
26: Jas 4, 4.
27–36: Mt 5, 38–48.
27: Prv 25, 21; Rom 12, 20–21.
28: Rom 12, 14; 1 Pt 3, 9.
31: Mt 7, 12.
34: Dt 15, 7–8.
35: Lv 25, 35–36.
37–42: Mt 7, 1–5.
37: Mt 6, 14; Jas 2, 13.
38: Mk 4, 24.
39: Mt 15, 14; 23, 16–17.24.
40: Mt 10, 24–25; Jn 13, 16; 15, 20.
43–45: Mt 7, 16–20; 12, 33.35.
46: Mt 7, 21; Rom 2, 13; Jas 1, 22.
47–49: Mt 7, 24–27.

†Chapter Six Footnotes

6, 1–11: The two episodes recounted here deal with gathering grain and healing, both of which were forbidden on the sabbath. In his defense of his disciples' conduct and his own charitable deed, Jesus argues that satisfying human needs such as hunger and performing works of mercy take precedence even over the sacred sabbath rest. See also the notes on Mt 12, 1–14 and Mk 2, 25–26.

6, 4: *The bread of offering:* see the note on Mt 12, 5–6.

6, 12–16: See the notes on Mt 10, 1—11, 1 and Mk 3, 14–15.

6, 12: *Spent the night in prayer:* see the note on 3, 21.

6, 13: *He chose Twelve:* the identification of this group as the *Twelve* is a part of early Christian tradition (see 1 Cor 15, 5), and in Mt and Lk, the Twelve are associated with the twelve tribes of Israel (22, 29–30; Mt 19, 28). After the fall of Judas from his position among the Twelve, the need is felt on the part of the early community to reconstitute this group before the Christian mission begins at Pentecost (Acts 1, 15–26). From Luke's perspective, they are an important group who because of their association with Jesus from the time of his baptism to his ascension (Acts 1, 21–22) provide the continuity between the historical Jesus and the church of Luke's day and who as the original eyewitnesses guarantee the fidelity of the church's beliefs and practices to the teachings of Jesus (1, 1–4). *Whom he also named apostles:* only Luke among the gospel writers attributes to Jesus the bestowal of the name *apostles* upon the Twelve. See the note on Mt 10, 2–4. "Apostle" becomes a technical term in early Christianity for a missionary sent out to preach the word of God. Although Luke seems to want to restrict the title to the Twelve (only in Acts 4, 4.14 are Paul and Barnabas termed apostles), other places in the New Testament show an awareness that the term was more widely applied (1 Cor 15, 5–7; Gal 1, 19; 1 Cor 1, 1; 9, 1; Rom 16, 7).

6, 14: *Simon, whom he named Peter:* see the note on Mk 3, 16.

6, 15: *Simon who was called a Zealot:* the Zealots were the instigators of the First Revolt of Palestinian Jews against Rome in A.D. 66–70. Because the existence of the Zealots as a distinct group during the lifetime of Jesus is the subject of debate, the meaning of the identification of Simon as a Zealot is unclear.

6, 16: *Judas Iscariot:* the name *Iscariot* may mean "man from Kerioth."

6, 17: *The coastal region of Tyre and Sidon:* not only Jews from Judea and Jerusalem, but even Gentiles from outside Palestine come to hear Jesus (see 2, 31–32; 3, 6; 4, 24–27).

6, 20–49: Luke's "Sermon on the Plain" is the counterpart to Mt's "Sermon on the Mount" (Mt 5, 1—7, 27). It is addressed to the disciples of Jesus, and, like the sermon in Mt, it begins with beatitudes (20–22) and ends with the parable of the two houses (46–49). Almost all the words of Jesus reported by Lk are found in Mt's version, but because Mt includes sayings that were related to specifically Jewish Christian problems (e.g., Mt 5, 17–20; 6, 1–8.16–18) that Luke did not find appropriate for his predominantly Gentile Christian audience, the "Sermon on the Mount" is considerably longer. Lk's sermon may be outlined as follows: an introduction consisting of blessings and woes (20–26); the love of one's enemies (27–36); the demands of loving one's neighbor (37–42); good deeds as proof of one's goodness (43–45); a parable illustrating the result of listening to and acting on the words of Jesus (46–49). At the core of the sermon is Jesus' teaching on the love of one's enemies (27–36) that has as its source of motivation God's graciousness and compassion for all humanity (35–36) and Jesus' teaching on the love of one's neighbor (37–42) that is characterized by forgiveness and generosity.

6, 20–26: The introductory portion of the sermon consists of blessings and woes that address the real economic and social conditions of humanity (the poor—the rich; the hungry—the satisfied; those grieving—those laughing; the outcast—the socially acceptable). By contrast, Matthew emphasizes the religious and spiritual values of disciples in the kingdom inaugurated by Jesus ("poor in spirit," 5, 5; "hunger and thirst for righteousness" 5, 6). In the sermon, *blessed* extols the fortunate condition of persons who are favored with the blessings of God; the woes, addressed as they are to the disciples of Jesus, threaten God's profound displeasure on those so blinded by their present fortunate situation that they do not recognize and appreciate the real values of God's kingdom. In all the blessings and woes, the present condition of the persons addressed will be reversed in the future.

6, 27–36: See the notes on Mt 5, 43–48 and 5, 48.

6, 37–42: See the notes on Mt 7, 1–12; 7, 1; 7, 5.

6, 43–46: See the notes on Mt 7, 15–20 and 12, 33.

6, 47–49: See the note on Mt 7, 24–27.

*Chapter Seven References

7, 1–10: Mt 8, 5–13; Jn 4, 43–54.

11–17: 4, 25–26; 1 Kgs 17, 17–24.

12: 8, 42; 1 Kgs 17, 17.

15: 1 Kgs 17, 23; 2 Kgs 4, 36.

16: 1, 68; 19, 44.

18–23: Mt 11, 2–6.

19: Mal 3, 1; Rv 1, 4.8; 4, 8.

22: 4, 18; Is 35, 5–6; 61, 1.

24–30: Mt 11, 7–15.

26: 1, 76.

27: Mal 3, 1 / Is 40, 3.

29–30: 3, 7.12; Mt 21, 32.

31–35: Mt 11, 16–19.

34: 15, 2.

36: 11, 37; 14, 1.

37: Mt 26, 7; Mk 14, 3.

37–38: Jn 12, 3.

48: 5, 20; Mt 9, 20; Mk 2, 5.

49: 5, 21.

†Chapter Seven Footnotes

7, 1—8, 3: The episodes in this section present a series of reactions to the Galilean ministry of Jesus and reflect some of Luke's particular interests: the faith of a Gentile (1–10); the prophet Jesus' concern for a widowed mother (11–17); the ministry of Jesus directed to the afflicted and unfortunate of Is 61, 1 (18–23); the relation between John and Jesus and their role in God's plan for salvation (24–35); a forgiven sinner's manifestation of love (36–50); the association of women with the ministry of Jesus (8, 1–3).

7, 1–10: This story about the faith of the centurion, a Gentile who cherishes the Jewish nation (5), prepares for the story in Acts of the conversion by Peter of the Roman centurion Cornelius who is similarly described as one who is generous to the Jewish nation (Acts 10, 2). See also Acts 10, 34–35 in the speech of Peter: "God shows no partiality . . . the person who fears him and acts righteously is acceptable to him." See also the notes on Mt 8, 5–13 and Jn 4, 43–54.

7, 2: *A centurion:* see the note on Mt 8, 5.

7, 6: *I am not worthy to have you enter under my roof:* to enter the house of a Gentile was considered unclean for a Jew; cf Acts 10, 28.

7, 11–17: In the previous incident Jesus' power was displayed for a Gentile whose servant was dying; in this episode it is displayed toward a widowed mother whose only son has already died. Jesus' power over death prepares for his reply to John's disciples in v 22: "the dead are raised." This resuscitation in alluding to the prophet Elijah's resurrection of the only son of a widow of Zarephath (1 Kgs 7, 18–24) leads to the reaction of the crowd: "A great prophet has arisen in our midst" (16).

7, 18–23: In answer to John's question, *Are you the one who is to come?*—a probable reference to the return of the fiery prophet of reform, Elijah, "before the day of the Lord comes, the great and terrible day" (Mal 3, 23)—Jesus responds that his role is rather to bring the blessings spoken of in Is 61, 1 to the oppressed and neglected of society (22; cf 4, 18).

7, 23: *Blessed is the one who takes no offense at me:* this beatitude is pronounced on the person who recognizes Jesus' true identity in spite of previous expectations of what "the one who is to come" would be like.

7, 24–30: In his testimony to John, Jesus reveals his understanding of the relationship between them: John is the precursor of Jesus (27); John is the messenger spoken of in Mal 3, 1 who in Mal 3, 23 is identified as Elijah. Taken with the previous episode, it can be seen that Jesus identifies John as precisely the person John envisioned Jesus to be: the Elijah who prepares the way for the coming of the day of the Lord.

7, 31–35: See the note on Mt 11, 16–19.

7, 36–50: In this story of the pardoning of the sinful woman Luke presents two different reactions to the ministry of Jesus. A Pharisee, suspecting Jesus to be a prophet, invites Jesus to a festive banquet in his house, but the Pharisee's self-righteousness leads to little forgiveness by God and consequently little love shown toward Jesus. The sinful woman, on the other hand, manifests a faith in God (50) that has led her to seek forgiveness for her sins, and because so much was forgiven, she now overwhelms Jesus with her display of love; cf the similar contrast in attitudes in 18, 9–14. The whole episode is a powerful lesson on the relation between forgiveness and love.

7, 36: *Reclined at table:* the normal posture of guests at a banquet. Other oriental banquet customs alluded to in this story include the reception by the host with a kiss (45), washing the feet of the guests (44), and the anointing of the guests' heads (46).

7, 41: *Days' wages:* one denarius is the normal daily wage of a laborer.

7, 47: *Her many sins have been forgiven; hence, she has shown great love:* literally, "her many sins have been forgiven, seeing that she has loved much." That the woman's sins have been forgiven is attested by the great love she shows toward Jesus. Her love is the consequence of her forgiveness. This is also the meaning demanded by the parable in vv 41–43.

*Chapter Eight References

8, 1: 4, 43.	17: 12, 2; Mt 10, 26.
2–3: 23, 49; 24, 10;	18: 19, 26; Mt 13,
Mt 27, 55–56;	12; 25, 29.
Mk 15, 40–41; Jn	19–21: Mt 12, 46–50;
19, 5.	Mk 3, 31–35.
4–8: Mt 13, 1–9; Mk	20–21: 11, 27–28.
4, 1–9.	22–25: Mt 8, 18.23–27;
8: 14, 35; Mt 11,	Mk 4, 35–41.
15; 13, 43; Mk 4,	26–39: Mt 8, 28–34; Mk
23.	5, 1–20.
9–10: Mt 13, 10–13;	28–29: 4, 33–35; Mt 8,
Mk 4, 10–12.	29; Mk 1, 23–24.
10: Is 6, 9.	40–56: Mt 9, 18–26; Mk
11–15: Mt 13, 18–23;	5, 21–43.
Mk 4, 13–20.	46: 6, 19.
11: 1 Pt 1, 23.	48: 7, 50; 17, 19; 18,
16–18: Mk 4, 21–25.	42.
16: 11, 33; Mt 5, 15.	52: 7, 13.

†Chapter Eight Footnotes

8, 1–3: Luke presents Jesus as an itinerant preacher traveling in the company of the Twelve and of the Galilean women who are sustaining them out of their means. These Galilean women will later accompany Jesus on his journey to Jerusalem and become witnesses to his death (23, 49) and resurrection (24, 9–11, where Mary Magdalene and Joanna are specifically mentioned; cf also Acts 1, 14). The association of women with the ministry of Jesus is most unusual in the light of the attitude of first-century Palestinian Judaism toward women. The more common attitude is expressed in Jn 4, 27, and early rabbinic documents caution against speaking with women in public.

8, 4–21: The focus in this section is on how one should hear the word of God and act on it. It includes the parable of the sower and its explanation (4–15), a collection of sayings on how one should act on the word that is heard (16–18), and the identification of the mother and brothers of Jesus as the ones who hear the word and act on it (19–21). See also the notes on Mt 13, 1–53 and Mk 4, 1–34.

8, 4–8: See the note on Mt 13, 3–8.

8, 11–15: On the interpretation of the parable of the sower, see the note on Mt 13, 18–23.

8, 16–18: These sayings continue the theme of responding to the word of God. Those who hear the word must become a light to others (16); even the mysteries of the kingdom that have been made known to the disciples (9–10) must come to light (17); a generous and persevering response to the word of God leads to a still more perfect response to the word.

8, 19: *His brothers:* see the note on Mk 6, 3.

8, 21: The family of Jesus is not constituted by physical relationship with him but by obedience to the word of God. In this, Luke agrees with the Marcan parallel (3, 31–35), although by omitting Mk 3, 33 and especially Mk 3, 20–21 Luke has softened the Marcan picture of Jesus' natural family. Probably he did this because Mary has already been presented in 1, 38 as the obedient handmaid of the Lord who fulfills the requirement for belonging to the eschatological family of Jesus; cf also 11, 27–28.

8, 22–56: This section records four miracles of Jesus that manifest his power and authority: (1) the calming of a storm on the lake (22–25); (2) the exorcism of a demoniac (26–39); (3) the cure of a hemorrhaging woman (40–48); (4) the raising of Jairus's daughter to life (49–56). They parallel the same sequence of stories at Mk 4, 35—5, 43.

8, 26: *Gerasenes:* other manuscripts read Gadarenes or Gergesenes. See also the note on Mt 8, 28. *Opposite Galilee:* probably Gentile territory (note the presence in

the area of pigs—unclean animals to Jews) and an indication that the person who receives salvation (36) is a Gentile.

8, 30: *What is your name?:* the question reflects the popular belief that knowledge of the spirit's name brought control over the spirit. *Legion:* to Jesus' question the demon replies with a Latin word transliterated into Greek. The Roman legion at this period consisted of 5,000 to 6,000 foot soldiers; hence the name implies a very large number of demons.

8, 31: *Abyss:* the place of the dead (Rom 10, 7) or the prison of Satan (Rv 20, 3) or the subterranean "watery deep" that symbolizes the chaos before the order imposed by creation (Gn 1, 2).

8, 35: *Sitting at his feet:* the former demoniac takes the position of a disciple before the master (10, 39; Acts 22, 3).

8, 40–56: Two interwoven miracle stories, one a healing and the other a resuscitation, present Jesus as master over sickness and death. In the Lucan account, faith in Jesus is responsible for the cure (48) and for the raising to life (50).

8, 42: *An only daughter:* cf the son of the widow of Nain whom Luke describes as an "only" son (7, 12; see also 9, 38).

8, 43: *Afflicted with hemorrhages for twelve years:* according to the Mosaic law (Lv 15, 25–30) this condition would render the woman unclean and unfit for contact with other people.

8, 52: *Sleeping:* her death is a temporary condition; cf Jn 11, 11–14.

*Chapter Nine References

9, 1–6: Mt 10, 1.5–15;	28–36: Mt 17, 1–8; Mk
Mk 6, 7–13.	9, 2–8.
4: 10, 5–7.	31: 9, 22; 13, 33.
5: 10, 10–11; Acts	32: Jn 1, 14; 2 Pt 1,
13, 51.	16.
7–9: Mt 14, 1–12; Mk	35: 3, 22; Dt 18, 15;
6, 14–29.	Ps 2, 7; Is 42, 1;
7–8: 9, 19; Mt 16, 14;	Mt 3, 17; 12, 18;
Mk 8, 28.	Mk 1, 11; 2 Pt 1,
9: 23, 8.	17–18.
10–17: Mt 14, 13–21;	37–43: Mt 17, 14–18;
Mk 6, 30–44; Jn	Mk 9, 14–27.
6, 1–14.	43–45: 18, 32–34; Mt
13–17: 2 Kgs 4, 42–44.	17, 22–23; Mk 9,
16: 22, 19; 24,	30–32.
30–31; Acts 2,	46–48: Mt 18, 1–5; Mk
42; 20, 11; 27,	9, 33–37.
35.	46: 22, 24.
18–21: Mt 16, 13–20;	48: 10, 16; Mt 10,
Mk 8, 27–30.	40; Jn 13, 20.
19: 9, 7–8.	49–50: Mk 9, 38–40.
22: 24, 7.26; Mt 16,	51: 9, 53; 13, 22.33;
21; 20, 18–19;	17, 11; 18, 31;
Mk 8, 31; 10,	19, 28; 24, 51;
33–34.	Acts 1,
23–27: Mt 16, 24–28;	2.9–11.22.
Mk 8, 34—9, 1.	52: Mal 3, 1.
23: 14, 27; Mt 10,	54: 2 Kgs 1, 10.12.
38.	57–60: Mt 8, 19–22.
24: 17, 33; Mt 10,	61–62: 1 Kgs 19, 20.
39; Jn 12, 25.	
26: 12, 9; Mt 10, 33;	
2 Tm 2, 12.	

†Chapter Nine Footnotes

9, 1–6: Armed with the power and authority that Jesus himself has been displaying in the previous episodes, the Twelve are now sent out to continue the work that Jesus has been performing throughout his Galilean ministry: (1) proclaiming the kingdom (4, 43; 8, 1); (2)

exorcising demons (4, 33–37.41; 8, 26–39) and (3) healing the sick (4, 38–40; 5, 12–16.17–26; 6, 6–10; 7, 1–10.17.22; 8, 40–56).

9, 3: *Take nothing for the journey:* the absolute detachment required of the disciple (14, 33) leads to complete reliance on God (12, 22–31).

9, 5: *Shake the dust from your feet:* see the note on Mt 10, 14.

9, 7–56: This section in which Luke gathers together incidents that focus on the identity of Jesus is introduced by a question that Herod is made to ask in this gospel: "Who then is this about whom I hear such things?" (9). In subsequent episodes, Luke reveals to the reader various answers to Herod's question: Jesus is one in whom God's power is present and who provides for the needs of God's people (10–17); Peter declares Jesus to be "the Messiah of God" (18–21); Jesus says he is the suffering Son of Man (22.43–45); Jesus is the Master to be followed, even to death (23–27); Jesus is God's Son, his Chosen One (28–36).

9, 7: *Herod the tetrarch:* see the note on 3, 1.

9, 9: *And he kept trying to see him:* this indication of Herod's interest in Jesus prepares for 13, 31–33 and for 23, 8–12 where Herod's curiosity about Jesus' power to perform miracles remains unsatisfied.

9, 16: *Then taking . . . :* the actions of Jesus recall the institution of the Eucharist in 22, 19; see also the note on Mt 14, 19.

9, 18–22: This incident is based on Mk 8, 27–33, but Luke has eliminated Peter's refusal to accept Jesus as suffering Son of Man (Mk 8, 32) and the rebuke of Peter by Jesus (Mk 8, 33). Elsewhere in the gospel, Luke softens the harsh portrait of Peter and the other apostles found in his Marcan source (cf 22, 39–46, which similarly lacks a rebuke of Peter that occurs in the source, Mk 14, 37–38).

9, 18: *When Jesus was praying in solitude:* see the note on 3, 21.

9, 20: *The Messiah of God:* on the meaning of this title in first-century Palestinian Judaism, see the notes on 2, 11 and on Mt 16, 13–20 and Mk 8, 27–30.

9, 23: *Daily:* this is a Lucan addition to a saying of Jesus, removing the saying from a context that envisioned the imminent suffering and death of the disciple of Jesus (as does the saying in Mk 8, 34–35) to one that focuses on the demands of daily Christian existence.

9, 28–36: Situated shortly after the first announcement of the passion, death, and resurrection, this scene of Jesus' transfiguration provides the heavenly confirmation to Jesus' declaration that his suffering will end in glory (32); see also the notes on Mt 17, 1–8 and Mk 9, 2–8.

9, 28: *Up the mountain to pray:* the "mountain" is the regular place of prayer in Lk (see 6, 12; 22, 39–41).

9, 30: *Moses and Elijah:* the two figures represent the Old Testament law and the prophets. At the end of this episode, the heavenly voice will identify Jesus as the one to be listened to now (35). See also the note on Mk 9, 5.

9, 31: *His exodus that he was going to accomplish in Jerusalem:* Luke identifies the subject of the conversation as the *exodus* of Jesus, a reference to the death, resurrection, and ascension of Jesus that will take place in Jerusalem, the city of destiny (see 9, 51). The mention of *exodus,* however, also calls to mind the Israelite Exodus from Egypt to the promised land.

9, 32: *They saw his glory:* the glory that is proper to God is here attributed to Jesus (see 24, 26).

9, 33: *Let us make three tents:* in a possible allusion to the feast of Tabernacles, Peter may be likening his joy on the occasion of the transfiguration to the joyful celebration of this harvest festival.

9, 34: *Over them:* it is not clear whether *them* refers to Jesus, Moses, and Elijah, or to the disciples. For the cloud casting its shadow, see the note on Mk 9, 7.

9, 35: Like the heavenly voice that identified Jesus at his baptism prior to his undertaking the Galilean ministry (3, 22), so too here before the journey to the city of destiny is begun (51) the heavenly voice again identifies Jesus as Son. *Listen to him:* the two representatives of Israel of old depart (33) and Jesus is left alone (36) as the teacher whose words must be heeded (see also Acts 3, 22).

9, 36: *At that time:* i.e., before the resurrection.

9, 37–43a: See the note on Mk 9, 14–29.

9, 46–50: These two incidents focus on attitudes that are opposed to Christian discipleship: rivalry and intolerance of outsiders.

9, 51—18, 14: The Galilean ministry of Jesus finishes with the previous episode and a new section of Luke's gospel begins, the journey to Jerusalem. This journey is based on Mk 10, 1–52, but Luke uses his Marcan source only in 18, 15—19, 27. Before that point he has inserted into his gospel a distinctive collection of sayings of Jesus and stories about him that he has drawn from Q, a collection of sayings of Jesus used also by Matthew, and from his own special traditions. All of the material collected in this section is loosely organized within the framework of a journey of Jesus to Jerusalem, the city of destiny, where his exodus (suffering, death, resurrection, ascension) is to take place (9, 31), where salvation is accomplished, and from where the proclamation of God's saving word is to go forth (24, 47; Acts 1, 8). Much of the material in the Lucan travel narrative is teaching for the disciples. During the course of this journey Jesus is preparing his chosen Galilean witnesses for the role they will play after his exodus (9, 31): they are to be his witnesses to the people (Acts 10, 39; 13, 31) and thereby provide certainty to the readers of Luke's gospel that the teachings they have received are rooted in the teachings of Jesus (1, 1–4).

9, 51–55: Just as the Galilean ministry began with a rejection of Jesus in his hometown, so too the travel narrative begins with the rejection of him by Samaritans. In this episode Jesus disassociates himself from the attitude expressed by his disciples that those who reject him are to be punished severely. The story alludes to 2 Kgs 1, 10.12, where the prophet Elijah takes the course of action Jesus rejects, and Jesus thereby rejects the identification of himself with Elijah.

9, 51: *Days for his being taken up:* like the reference to his exodus in v 31, this is probably a reference to all the events (suffering, death, resurrection, ascension) of his last days in Jerusalem. *He resolutely determined:* literally, "he set his face."

9, 52: *Samaritan:* Samaria was the territory between Judea and Galilee west of the Jordan river. For ethnic and religious reasons, the Samaritans and the Jews were bitterly opposed to one another (see Jn 4, 9).

9, 57–62: In these sayings Jesus speaks of the severity and the unconditional nature of Christian discipleship. Even family ties and filial obligations, such as burying one's parents, cannot distract one no matter how briefly from proclaiming the kingdom of God. The first two sayings are paralleled in Mt 8, 19–22; see also the notes there.

9, 60: *Let the dead bury their dead:* i.e., let the spiritually dead (those who do not follow) bury their physically dead. See also the note on Mt 8, 22.

*Chapter Ten References

10, 1:	Mk 6, 7.
2:	Mt 9, 37–38; Jn 4, 35.
3:	Mt 10, 16.
4:	9, 3; 2 Kgs 4, 29.
4–11:	Mt 10, 7–14.
7:	9, 4; Mt 10, 10; 1 Cor 9, 6–14; 1 Tm 5, 18.
8:	1 Cor 10, 27.
9:	Mt 3, 2; 4, 17; Mk 1, 15.
10–11:	9, 5.
11:	Acts 13, 51; 18, 6.
12:	Mt 10, 15; 11, 24.
13–15:	Mt 11, 20–24.
13–14:	Is 23; Ez 26–28; Jl 3, 4–8; Am 1, 1–10; Zec 9, 2–4.
15:	Is 14, 13–15.
16:	Mt 10, 40; Jn 5, 23; 13, 20; 15, 23.
18:	Is 14, 12; Jn 12, 31; Rv 12, 7–12.
19:	Ps 19, 13; Mk 16, 18.
20:	Ex 32, 32; Dn 12, 1; Mt 7, 22; Phil 4, 3; Heb 12, 23; Rv 3, 5; 21, 27.
21–22:	Mt 11, 25–27.
21:	1 Cor 1, 26–28.
22:	Jn 3, 35; 10, 15.
23–24:	Mt 13, 16–17.
25–28:	Mt 22, 34–40; Mk 12, 28–34.
25:	18, 18; Mt 19, 16; Mk 10, 17.
27:	Lv 19, 18; Dt 6, 5; 10, 12; Jos 22, 5; Mt 19, 19; 22, 37–39; Rom 13, 9; Gal 5, 14; Jas 2, 8.
28:	Lv 18, 5; Prv 19, 16; Rom 10, 5; Gal 3, 12.
38–39:	Jn 11, 1; 12, 2–3.

†Chapter Ten Footnotes

10, 1–12: Only the Gospel of Luke contains two episodes in which Jesus sends out his followers on a mission: the first (9, 1–6) is based on the mission in Mk 6, 6b–13 and recounts the sending out of the Twelve; here in vv 1–12 a similar report based on Q becomes the sending out of seventy-two in this gospel. The episode continues the theme of Jesus preparing witnesses to himself and his ministry. These witnesses include not only the Twelve but also the seventy-two who may represent the Christian mission in Luke's own day. Note that the instructions given to the Twelve and to the seventy-two are similar and that what is said to the seventy-two in v 4 is directed to the Twelve in 22, 35.

10, 1: *Seventy[-two]:* important representatives of the Alexandrian and Caesarean text types read "seventy," while other important Alexandrian texts and Western readings have "seventy-two."

10, 4: *Carry no money bag . . . greet no one along the way:* because of the urgency of the mission and the single-mindedness required of missionaries, attachment to material possessions should be avoided and even customary greetings should not distract from the fulfillment of the task.

10, 5: *First say, 'Peace to this household':* see the notes on 2, 14 and Mt 10, 13.

10, 6: *A peaceful person:* literally, "a son of peace."

10, 13–16: The call to repentance that is a part of the proclamation of the kingdom brings with it a severe judgment for those who hear it and reject it.

10, 15: *The netherworld:* the underworld, the place of the dead (Acts 2, 27.31), here contrasted with heaven; see also the note on Mt 11, 23.

10, 18: *I have observed Satan fall like lightning:* the effect of the mission of the seventy-two is characterized by the Lucan Jesus as a symbolic fall of Satan. As the kingdom of God is gradually being established, evil in all its forms is being defeated; the dominion of Satan over humanity is at an end.

10, 21: *Revealed them to the childlike:* a restatement of the theme announced in 8, 10: the mysteries of the kingdom are revealed to the disciples. See also the note on Mt 11, 25–27.

10, 25–37: In response to a question from a Jewish le-

gal expert about inheriting eternal life, Jesus illustrates the superiority of love over legalism through the story of the good Samaritan. The law of love proclaimed in the "Sermon on the Plain" (6, 27–36) is exemplified by one whom the legal expert would have considered ritually impure (see Jn 4, 9). Moreover, the identity of the "neighbor" requested by the legal expert (29) turns out to be a Samaritan, the enemy of the Jew (see the note on 9, 52).

10, 25: *Scholar of the law:* an expert in the Mosaic law, and probably a member of the group elsewhere identified as the scribes (5, 21).

10, 31–32: *Priest . . . Levite:* those religious representatives of Judaism who would have been expected to be models of "neighbor" to the victim pass him by.

10, 38–42: The story of Martha and Mary further illustrates the importance of hearing the words of the teacher and the concern with women in Lk.

10, 39: *Sat beside the Lord at his feet:* it is remarkable for first-century Palestinian Judaism that a woman would assume the posture of a disciple at the master's feet (see also 8, 35; Acts 22, 3), and it reveals a characteristic attitude of Jesus toward women in this gospel (see 8, 2–3).

10, 42: *There is need of only one thing:* some ancient versions read, "there is need of few things"; another important, although probably inferior, reading found in some manuscripts is, "there is need of few things, or of one."

*Chapter Eleven References

11, 1–4:	Mt 6, 9–15.
5–8:	18, 1–5.
9–13:	Mt 7, 7–11.
9:	Mt 21, 22; Mk 11, 24; Jn 14, 13; 15, 7; 1 Jn 5, 14–15.
14–23:	Mt 12, 22–30; Mk 3, 20–27.
15:	Mt 9, 34.
16:	Mt 12, 38; 16, 1; Mk 8, 11; 1 Cor 1, 22.
20:	Ex 8, 19.
23:	9, 50; Mk 9, 40.
24–26:	Mt 12, 43–45.
26:	Jn 5, 14.
27:	1, 28.42.48.
29–32:	Mt 12, 38–42; Mk 8, 12.
29:	Mt 16, 1.4; Jn 6, 30; 1 Cor 1, 22.
31:	1 Kgs 10, 1–10; 2 Chr 9, 1–12.
32:	Jon 3, 8.10.
33:	8, 16; Mt 5, 15; Mk 4, 21.
34–36:	Mt 6, 22–23.
37–54:	20, 45–47; Mt 23, 1–36; Mk 12, 38–40.
37:	7, 36; 14, 1.
38:	Mt 15, 2; Mk 7, 2–5.
39–41:	Mt 23, 25–26.
42:	Lv 27, 30; Mt 23, 23.
43:	20, 46; Mt 23, 6; Mk 12, 38–39.
44:	Mt 23, 27.
45:	Mt 23, 4.
47–48:	Mt 23, 29–32.
49–51:	Mt 23, 34–36.
51:	Gn 4, 8; 2 Chr 24, 20–22.
52:	Mt 23, 13.
53:	6, 11; Mt 22, 15–22.
54:	20, 20.

†Chapter Eleven Footnotes

11, 1–13: Luke presents three episodes concerned with prayer. The first (1–4) recounts Jesus teaching his disciples the Christian communal prayer, the "Our Father"; the second (5–8), the importance of persistence in prayer; the third (9–13), the effectiveness of prayer.

11, 1–4: The Matthean form of the "Our Father" occurs in the "Sermon on the Mount" (Mt 6, 9–15); the shorter Lucan version is presented while Jesus is at prayer (see the note on 3, 21) and his disciples ask him to teach them to pray just as John taught his disciples to pray. In answer to their question, Jesus presents them with an example of a Christian communal prayer that stresses the fatherhood of God and acknowledges him as the one to whom the Christian disciple owes daily sustenance (3), forgiveness (4), and deliverance from the final trial (4). See also the notes on Mt 6, 9–13.

11, 2: *Your kingdom come:* in place of this petition, some early church Fathers record: "May your holy Spirit come upon us and cleanse us," a petition that may reflect the use of the "Our Father" in a baptismal liturgy.

11, 3–4: *Daily bread:* see the note on Mt 6, 11. *The final test:* see the note on Mt 6, 13.

11, 13: *The holy Spirit:* this is a Lucan editorial alteration of a traditional saying of Jesus (see Mt 7, 11). Luke presents the gift of the holy Spirit as the response of the Father to the prayer of the Christian disciple.

11, 19: *Your own people:* the Greek reads "your sons." Other Jewish exorcists (see Acts 19, 13–20), who recognize that the power of God is active in the exorcism, would themselves convict the accusers of Jesus. See also the note on Mt 12, 27.

11, 22: *One stronger:* i.e., Jesus. Cf 3, 16 where John the Baptist identifies Jesus as "more powerful than I."

11, 27–28: The beatitude in v 28 should not be interpreted as a rebuke of the mother of Jesus; see the note on 8, 21. Rather, it emphasizes (like 2, 35) that attentiveness to God's word is more important than biological relationship to Jesus.

11, 29–32: The "sign of Jonah" in Lk is the preaching of the need for repentance by a prophet who comes from afar. Cf Mt 12, 38–42 (and see the notes there) where the "sign of Jonah" is interpreted by Jesus as his death and resurrection.

11, 37–54: This denunciation of the Pharisees (39–44) and the scholars of the law (45–52) is set by Luke in the context of Jesus' dining at the home of a Pharisee. Controversies with or reprimands of Pharisees are regularly set by Luke within the context of Jesus' eating with Pharisees (see 5, 29–39; 7, 36–50; 14, 1–24). A different compilation of similar sayings is found in Mt 23 (see also the notes there).

11, 44: *Unseen graves:* contact with the dead or with human bones or graves (see Nm 19, 16) brought ritual impurity. Jesus presents the Pharisees as those who insidiously lead others astray through their seeming attention to the law.

11, 45: *Scholars of the law:* see the note on 10, 25.

11, 49: *I will send to them prophets and apostles:* Jesus connects the mission of the church (apostles) with the mission of the Old Testament prophets who often suffered the rebuke of their contemporaries.

11, 51: *From the blood of Abel to the blood of Zechariah:* the murder of Abel is the first murder recounted in the Old Testament (Gn 4, 8). The Zechariah mentioned here may be the Zechariah whose murder is recounted in 2 Chr 24, 20–22, the last murder presented in the Hebrew canon of the Old Testament.

*Chapter Twelve References

12, 1:	Mt 16, 6; Mk 8, 15.	24:	12, 7.
2–9:	Mt 10, 26–33.	27:	1 Kgs 10, 4–7; 2 Chr 9, 3–6.
2:	8, 17; Mk 4, 22.	32:	22, 29; Rv 1, 6.
7:	12, 24; 21, 18; Acts 27, 34.	33:	18, 22; Mt 6, 20–21; Mk 10, 21.
9:	9, 26; Mk 8, 38; 2 Tm 2, 12.	35–46:	Mt 24, 45–51.
10:	Mt 12, 31–32; Mk 3, 28–29.	36:	Mt 25, 1–13; Mk 13, 35–37.
11–12:	21, 12–15; Mt 10, 17–20; Mk 13, 11.	39–40:	Mt 24, 43–44; 1 Thes 5, 2.
		47:	Jas 4, 17.
14:	Ex 2, 14; Acts 7, 27.	50:	Mk 10, 38–39.
15:	1 Tm 6, 9–10.	51–53:	Mt 10, 34–35.
19–21:	Mt 6, 19–21; 1 Tm 6, 17.	51:	2, 14.
		53:	Mi 7, 6.
19–20:	Sir 11, 19.	54–56:	Mt 16, 2–3.
22–32:	Mt 6, 25–34.	57–59:	Mt 5, 25–26.

†Chapter Twelve Footnotes

12, 1: See the notes on Mk 8, 15 and Mt 16, 5–12.

12, 2–9: Luke presents a collection of sayings of Jesus exhorting his followers to acknowledge him and his mission fearlessly and assuring them of God's protection even in times of persecution. They are paralleled in Mt 10, 26–33.

12, 5: *Gehenna:* see the note on Mt 5, 22.

12, 6: *Two small coins:* the Roman copper coin, the assarion (Latin *as*), was worth about one-sixteenth of a denarius (see the note on 7, 41).

12, 10–12: The sayings about the holy Spirit are set in the context of fearlessness in the face of persecution (2–9; cf Mt 12, 31–32). The holy Spirit will be present in Luke's second volume, the Acts of the Apostles, as the power responsible for the guidance of the Christian mission and the source of courage in the face of persecution.

12, 13–34: Luke has joined together sayings contrasting those whose focus and trust in life is on material possessions, symbolized here by the rich fool of the parable (16–21), with those who recognize their complete dependence on God (21), those whose radical detachment from material possessions symbolizes their heavenly treasure (33–34).

12, 21: *Rich in what matters to God:* literally, "rich for God."

12, 35–48: This collection of sayings relates to Luke's understanding of the end time and the return of Jesus. Luke emphasizes for his readers the importance of being faithful to the instructions of Jesus in the period before the parousia.

12, 45: *My master is delayed in coming:* this statement indicates that early Christian expectations for the imminent return of Jesus had undergone some modification. Luke cautions his readers against counting on such a delay and acting irresponsibly. Cf the similar warning in Mt 24, 48.

12, 49–53: Jesus' proclamation of the kingdom is a refining and purifying fire. His message that meets with acceptance or rejection will be a source of conflict and dissension even within families.

12, 50: *Baptism:* i.e., his death.

12, 59: *The last penny:* Greek, *lepton,* a very small amount. Mt 5, 26 has for "the last penny" the Greek word *kodrantēs* (Latin *quadrans,* "farthing").

*Chapter Thirteen References

13, 2:	Jn 9, 2.	24–30:	Mt 7, 13–14.21–23.
3–5:	Jn 8, 24.		
6–9:	Jer 8, 13; Hb 3, 17; Mt 21, 19; Mk 11, 13.	24:	Mk 10, 25.
		25:	Mt 25, 10–12.
		27:	Ps 6, 9; Mt 7, 23; 25, 41.
14:	6, 7; 14, 3; Ex 20, 8–11; Dt 5, 12–15; Mt 12, 10; Mk 3, 2–4; Jn 5, 16; 7, 23; 9, 14.16.	28–29:	Mt 8, 11–12.
		29:	Ps 107, 2–3.
		30:	Mt 19, 20; 20, 16; Mk 10, 31.
15:	14, 5; Dt 22, 4; Mt 12, 11.	33:	2, 38; Jn 6, 30; 8, 20.
16:	19, 9.	34–35:	19, 41–44; Mt 23, 37–39.
18–19:	Mt 13, 31–32; Mk 4, 30–32.	35:	19, 38; 1 Kgs 9, 7–8; Ps 118, 26; Jer 7, 4–7.13–15; 12, 7; 22, 5.
19:	Ez 17, 23–24; 31, 6.		
20–21:	Mt 13, 33.		

†Chapter Thirteen Footnotes

13, 1–5: The death of the Galileans at the hands of Pilate (1) and the accidental death of those on whom the tower fell (4) are presented by the Lucan Jesus as timely reminders of the need for all to repent, for the victims of these tragedies should not be considered outstanding sinners who were singled out for punishment.

13, 1: The slaughter of the Galileans by Pilate is unknown outside Lk; but from what is known about Pilate from the Jewish historian Josephus, such a slaughter would be in keeping with the character of Pilate. Josephus reports that Pilate had disrupted a religious gathering of the Samaritans on Mt. Gerizim with a slaughter of the participants (*Antiquities* 18, 4, 1 §§86–87), and that on another occasion Pilate had killed many Jews who had opposed him when he appropriated money from the temple treasury to build an aqueduct in Jerusalem (*Jewish War* 2, 9, 4 §§175–77; *Antiquities* 18, 3, 2 §§60–62).

13, 4: Like the incident mentioned in v 1, nothing of this accident in Jerusalem is known outside Lk and the New Testament.

13, 6–9: Following on the call to repentance in vv 1–5, the parable of the barren fig tree presents a story about the continuing patience of God with those who have not yet given evidence of their repentance (see 3, 8). The parable may also be alluding to the delay of the end time, when punishment will be meted out, and the importance of preparing for the end of the age because the delay will not be permanent (8–9).

13, 10–17: The cure of the crippled woman on the sabbath and the controversy that results furnishes a parallel to an incident that will be reported by Lk in 14, 1–6, the cure of the man with dropsy on the sabbath. A characteristic of Luke's style is the juxtaposition of an incident that reveals Jesus' concern for a man with an incident that reveals his concern for a woman; cf, e.g., 7, 11–17 and 8, 49–56.

13, 15–16: If the law as interpreted by Jewish tradition allowed for the untying of bound animals on the sabbath, how much more should this woman who has been bound by Satan's power be freed on the sabbath from her affliction.

13, 16: *Whom Satan has bound:* affliction and infirmity are taken as evidence of Satan's hold on humanity. The healing ministry of Jesus reveals the gradual wresting from Satan of control over humanity and the establishment of God's kingdom.

13, 18–21: Two parables are used to illustrate the future proportions of the kingdom of God that will result from its deceptively small beginning in the preaching and healing ministry of Jesus. They are paralleled in Mt 13, 31–33 and Mk 4, 30–32.

13, 22–30: These sayings of Jesus follow in Lk upon the parables of the kingdom (18–21) and stress that great effort is required for entrance into the kingdom (24) and that there is an urgency to accept the present opportunity to enter because the narrow door will not remain open indefinitely (25). Lying behind the sayings is the rejection of Jesus and his message by his Jewish contemporaries (26) whose places at table in the kingdom will be taken by Gentiles from the four corners of the world (29). Those called last (the Gentiles) will precede those to whom the invitation to enter was first extended (the Jews). See also 14, 15–24.

13, 32: Nothing, not even Herod's desire to kill Jesus, stands in the way of Jesus' role in fulfilling God's will and in establishing the kingdom through his exorcisms and healings.

13, 33: *It is impossible that a prophet should die outside of Jerusalem:* Jerusalem is the city of destiny and the goal of the journey of the prophet Jesus. Only when he reaches the holy city will his work be accomplished.

*Chapter Fourteen References

14, 1–6:	6, 6–11; 13, 10–17.	16–24:	Mt 22, 2–10.
1:	11, 37.	26–27:	Mt 10, 37–38.
3:	6, 9; Mk 3, 4.	26:	9, 57–62; 18, 29; Jn 12, 25.
5:	13, 15; Dt 22, 4; Mt 12, 11.	27:	9, 23; Mt 16, 24; Mk 8, 34.
6:	Mt 22, 46.	33:	5, 11.
7:	11, 43; Mt 23, 6; Mk 12, 38–39.	34:	Mt 5, 13; Mk 9, 50.
8–10:	Prv 25, 6–7.	35:	8, 8; Mt 11, 15; 13, 9; Mk 4, 9.23.
11:	18, 14.		
12:	6, 32–35.		
14:	Jn 5, 29.		

†Chapter Fourteen Footnotes

14, 1–6: See the note on 13, 10–17.

14, 2: *Dropsy:* an abnormal swelling of the body because of the retention and accumulation of fluid.

14, 5: *Your son or ox:* this is the reading of many of the oldest and most important New Testament manuscripts. Because of the strange collocation of *son* and *ox,* some copyists have altered it to "your ass or ox," on the model of the saying in 13, 15.

14, 7–14: The banquet scene found only in Luke provides the opportunity for these teachings of Jesus on humility and presents a setting to display Luke's interest in Jesus' attitude toward the rich and the poor (see the notes on 4, 18; 6, 20–26; 12, 13–34).

14, 15–24: The parable of the great dinner is a further illustration of the rejection by Israel, God's chosen people, of Jesus' invitation to share in the banquet in the kingdom and the extension of the invitation to other Jews whose identification as the poor, crippled, blind, and lame (21) classifies them among those who recognize their need for salvation, and to Gentiles (23). A similar parable is found in Mt 22, 1–10.

14, 25–33: This collection of sayings, most of which are peculiar to Lk, focuses on the total dedication necessary for the disciple of Jesus. No attachment to family (26) or possessions (33) can stand in the way of the total commitment demanded of the disciple. Also, acceptance of the call to be a disciple demands readiness to accept persecution and suffering (27) and a realistic assessment of the hardships and costs (28–32).

14, 26: *Hating his father . . . :* cf the similar saying in Mt 10, 37. The disciple's family must take second place to the absolute dedication involved in following Jesus (see also 9, 59–62).

14, 34–35: The simile of salt follows the sayings of Jesus that demanded of the disciple total dedication and detachment from family and possessions and illustrates the condition of one who does not display this total commitment. The halfhearted disciple is like salt that cannot serve its intended purpose. See the simile of salt in Mt 5, 13 and the note there.

*Chapter Fifteen References

15, 1–7:	Mt 9, 10–13.	4:	Ez 34, 11–12.16.
2:	5, 30; 19, 7.	7:	Ez 18, 23.
4–7:	Mt 18, 12–14.	13:	Prv 29, 3.
4–6:	19, 10.		

†Chapter Fifteen Footnotes

15, 1–32: To the parable of the lost sheep (1–7) that Luke shares with Matthew (Mt 18, 12–14), Luke adds two parables (the lost coin, 8–10; the prodigal son, 11–32) from his own special tradition to illustrate Jesus' particular concern for the lost and God's love for the repentant sinner.

15, 8: *Ten coins:* literally, "ten drachmas." A drachma was a Greek silver coin.

*Chapter Sixteen References

16, 8:	Eph 5, 8; 1 Thes 5, 5.	18:	Mt 5, 32; 19, 9; Mk 10, 11–12;
9:	12, 33.		1 Cor 7, 10–11.
10:	19, 17; Mt 25, 20–23.	21:	Mt 15, 27; Mk 7, 28.
13:	Mt 6, 24.	25:	6, 24–25.
15:	18, 9–14.	31:	Jn 5, 46–47; 11, 44–48.
16:	Mt 11, 12–13.		
17:	Mt 5, 18.		

†Chapter Sixteen Footnotes

16, 1–8a: The parable of the dishonest steward has to be understood in the light of the Palestinian custom of agents acting on behalf of their masters and the usurious practices common to such agents. The dishonesty of the steward consisted in the squandering of his master's property (1) and not in any subsequent graft. The master commends the dishonest steward who has forgone his own usurious commission on the business transaction by having the debtors write new notes that reflected only the real amount owed the master (i.e., minus the steward's profit). The dishonest steward acts in this way in order to ingratiate himself with the debtors because he knows he is being dismissed from his position (3). The parable, then, teaches the prudent use of one's material goods in light of an imminent crisis.

16, 6: *One hundred measures:* literally, "one hundred *baths*." A *bath* is a Hebrew unit of liquid measurement equivalent to eight or nine gallons.

16, 7: *One hundred kors:* a *kor* is a Hebrew unit of dry measure for grain or wheat equivalent to ten or twelve bushels.

16, 8b–13: Several originally independent sayings of Jesus are gathered here by Luke to form the concluding application of the parable by the dishonest steward.

16, 8b–9: The first conclusion recommends the prudent use of one's wealth (in the light of the coming of the end of the age) after the manner of the children of this world, represented in the parable by the dishonest steward.

16, 9: *Dishonest wealth:* literally, "mammon of iniquity." Mammon is the Greek transliteration of a Hebrew or Aramaic word that is usually explained as meaning "that in which one trusts." The characterization of this wealth as *dishonest* expresses a tendency of wealth to lead one to dishonesty. *Eternal dwellings:* or, "eternal tents," i.e., heaven.

16, 10–12: The second conclusion recommends constant fidelity to those in positions of responsibility.

16, 13: The third conclusion is a general statement about the incompatibility of serving God and being a slave to riches. To be dependent upon wealth is opposed to the teachings of Jesus who counseled complete dependence on the Father as one of the characteristics of the Christian disciple (12, 22–39). *God and mammon:* see the note on 16, 9. Mammon is used here as if it were itself a god.

16, 14–18: The two parables about the use of riches in ch 16 are separated by several isolated sayings of Jesus on the hypocrisy of the Pharisees (14–15), on the law (16–17), and on divorce (18).

16, 14–15: The Pharisees are here presented as examples of those who are slaves to wealth (see 16, 13) and, consequently, they are unable to serve God.

16, 16: John the Baptist is presented in Luke's gospel as a transitional figure between the period of Israel, the time of promise, and the period of Jesus, the time of fulfillment. With John, the fulfillment of the Old Testament promises has begun.

16, 19–31: The parable of the rich man and Lazarus again illustrates Luke's concern with Jesus' attitude toward the rich and the poor. The reversal of the fates of the rich man and Lazarus (22–23) illustrates the teachings of Jesus in Luke's "Sermon on the Plain" (6, 20–21.24–25).

16, 19: The oldest Greek manuscript of Lk dating from ca. A.D. 175–225 records the name of the rich man as an abbreviated form of "Nineveh," but there is very little textual support in other manuscripts for this reading. "Dives" of popular tradition is the Latin Vulgate's translation for "rich man."

16, 23: *The netherworld:* see the note on 10, 15.

16, 30–31: A foreshadowing in Luke's gospel of the rejection of the call to repentance even after Jesus' resurrection.

*Chapter Seventeen References

17, 1–2:	Mt 18, 6–7.	24:	Mt 24, 27.
3:	Mt 18, 15.	25:	9, 22; 18, 32–33; Mt 16, 21; 17, 22–23; 20, 18–19; Mk 8, 31; 9, 31; 10, 33–34.
4:	Mt 6, 14; 18, 21–22.35; Mk 11, 25.		
6:	Mt 17, 20; 21, 21; Mk 11, 23.		
11:	9, 51–53; 13, 22.33; 18, 31; 19, 28; Jn 4, 4.	26–27:	Gn 6–8; Mt 24, 37–39.
		28–29:	Gn 18, 20–21; 19, 1–29.
13:	18, 38; Mt 9, 27; 15, 22.	31:	Mt 24, 17–18; Mk 13, 15–16.
14:	5, 14; Lv 14, 2–32; Mt 8, 4; Mk 1, 44.	31–32:	Gn 19, 17.26.
19:	7, 50; 18, 42.	33:	9, 24; Mt 10, 39; 16, 25; Mk 8, 35; Jn 12, 25.
20:	Jn 3, 3.		
21:	17, 23; Mt 24, 23; Mk 13, 21.	35:	Mt 24, 40–41.
23:	17, 21; Mt 24, 23.26; Mk 13, 21.	37:	Jb 39, 30; Mt 24, 28.

†Chapter Seventeen Footnotes

17, 3a: *Be on your guard:* the translation takes v 3a as the conclusion to the saying on scandal in vv 1–2. It is not impossible that it should be taken as the beginning of the saying on forgiveness in vv 3b–4.

17, 7–10: These sayings of Jesus, peculiar to Luke, which continue his response to the apostles' request to increase their faith (5–6), remind them that Christian disciples can make no claim on God's graciousness; in fulfilling the exacting demands of discipleship, they are only doing their duty.

17, 11–19: This incident recounting the thankfulness of the cleansed Samaritan leper is narrated only in Luke's gospel and provides an instance of Jesus holding up a non-Jew (18) as an example to his Jewish contemporaries (cf 10, 33 where a similar purpose is achieved in the story of the good Samaritan). Moreover, it is the faith in Jesus manifested by the foreigner that has brought him salvation (19; cf the similar relationship between faith and salvation in 7, 50; 8, 48.50).

17, 11: *Through Samaria and Galilee:* or, "between Samaria and Galilee."

17, 14: See the note on 5, 14.

17, 20–37: To the question of the Pharisees about the time of the coming of God's kingdom, Jesus replies that the kingdom is *among you* (20–21). The emphasis has thus been shifted from an imminent observable coming of the kingdom to something that is already present in Jesus' preaching and healing ministry. Luke has also appended further traditional sayings of Jesus about the unpredictable suddenness of the day of the Son of Man, and assures his readers that in spite of the delay of that day (12, 45), it will bring judgment unexpectedly on those who do not continue to be vigilant.

17, 21: *Among you:* the Greek preposition translated as *among* can also be translated as "within." In the light of other statements in Luke's gospel about the presence of the kingdom (see 10, 9.11; 11, 20) "among" is to be preferred.

17, 36: The inclusion of v 36, "There will be two men in the field; one will be taken, the other left behind," in some Western manuscripts appears to be a scribal assimilation to Mt 24, 40.

*Chapter Eighteen References

18, 1:	Rom 12, 12; Col 4, 2; 1 Thes 5, 17.	22:	12, 33; Sir 29, 11; Mt 6, 20.
5:	11, 8.	27:	Mk 14, 36.
9:	16, 5; Mt 23, 25–28.	29–30:	14, 26.
12:	Mt 23, 23.	31–34:	24, 25–27.44; Mt 20, 17–19; Mk 10, 32–34; Acts 3, 18.
13:	Ps 51, 3.		
14:	14, 11; Mt 23, 12.	32–33:	9, 22.44.
15–17:	Mt 19, 13–15; Mk 10, 13–16.	34:	Mk 9, 32.
		35–43:	Mt 20, 29–34; Mk 10, 46–52.
17:	Mt 18, 3.	38–39:	17, 13; Mt 9, 27; 15, 22.
18–30:	Mt 19, 16–30; Mk 10, 17–31.		
18:	10, 25.	41:	Mk 10, 36.
20:	Ex 20, 12–16; Dt 5, 16–20.	42:	7, 50; 17, 19.

†Chapter Eighteen Footnotes

18, 1–14: The particularly Lucan material in the travel narrative concludes with two parables on prayer. The first (1–8) teaches the disciples the need of persistent prayer so that they not fall victims to apostasy (8). The second (9–14) condemns the self-righteous, critical attitude of the Pharisee and teaches that the fundamental attitude of the Christian disciple must be the recognition of sinfulness and complete dependence on God's graciousness. The second parable recalls the story of the pardoning of the sinful woman (7, 36–50) where a similar contrast is presented between the critical attitude of the Pharisee Simon and the love shown by the pardoned sinner.

18, 5: *Strike me:* the Greek verb translated as *strike* means "to strike under the eye" and suggests the extreme situation to which the persistence of the widow might lead. It may, however, be used here in the much weaker sense of "to wear one out."

18, 15—19, 27: Luke here includes much of the material about the journey to Jerusalem found in his Marcan source (10, 1–52) and adds to it the story of Zacchaeus (19, 1–10) from his own particular tradition and the parable of the gold coins (minas) (19, 11–27) from Q, the source common to Lk and Mt.

18, 15–17: The sayings on children furnish a contrast to the attitude of the Pharisee in the preceding episode (9–14) and that of the wealthy official in the following one (18–23) who think that they can lay claim to God's favor by their own merit. The attitude of the disciple should be marked by the receptivity and trustful dependence characteristic of the child.

18, 22: Detachment from material possessions results in the total dependence on God demanded of one who would inherit eternal life. *Sell all that you have:* the original saying (cf Mk 10, 21) has characteristically been made more demanding by Luke's addition of "all."

18, 31–33: The details included in this third announcement of Jesus' suffering and death suggest that the literary formulation of the announcement has been directed by the knowledge of the historical passion and death of Jesus.

18, 31: *Everything written by the prophets . . . will be fulfilled:* this is a Lucan addition to the words of Jesus found in the Marcan source (Mk 10, 32–34). Luke understands the events of Jesus' last days in Jerusalem to be the fulfillment of Old Testament prophecy, but, as is usually the case in Luke-Acts, the author does not specify which Old Testament prophets he has in mind; cf 24, 25.27.44; Acts 3, 8; 13, 27; 26, 22–23.

18, 38: *Son of David:* the blind beggar identifies Jesus with a title that is related to Jesus' role as Messiah (see the note on 2, 11). Through this Son of David, salvation comes to the blind man. Note the connection between salvation and house of David mentioned earlier in Zechariah's canticle (1, 69). See also the note on Mt 9, 27.

*Chapter Nineteen References

19, 7:	5, 30; 15, 2.	42:	8, 10; Is 6, 9–10; Mt 13, 14; Mk 4, 12; Acts 28, 26–27; Rom 11, 8.10.
8:	Ex 21, 37; Nm 5, 6–7; 2 Sm 12, 6.		
9:	13, 16; Mt 21, 31.		
10:	15, 4–10; Ez 34, 16.	43:	Is 29, 3.
11–27:	Mt 25, 14–30.	44:	1, 68; 21, 6; Ps 137, 9; Mt 24, 2; Mk 13, 2.
12:	Mk 13, 34.		
17:	16, 10.	45–46:	Mt 21, 12–13; Mk 11, 15–17; Jn 2, 13–17.
26:	8, 18; Mt 13, 12; Mk 4, 25.		
28–40:	Mt 21, 1–11; Mk 11, 1–11; Jn 12, 12–19.	45:	Mal 3, 1 / Hos 9,15.
		46:	Is 56, 7; Jer 7, 11.
29:	Zec 14, 4.		
30:	Nm 19, 2; Dt 21, 3, 1 Sm 6, 7; Zec 9, 9.	47–48:	20, 19; 22, 2; Mt 21, 46; Mk 11, 18; 12, 12; 14, 1–2; Jn 5, 18; 7, 30.
32:	22, 13.		
35–36:	2 Kgs 9, 13.		
38:	2, 14; Ps 118, 26.	47:	21, 37; 22, 53; Jn 18, 20.
41–44:	13, 34–35.		
41:	2 Kgs 8, 11–12; Jer 14, 17; 15, 5.		

†Chapter Nineteen Footnotes

19, 1–10: The story of the tax collector Zacchaeus is unique to this gospel. While a rich man (2), Zacchaeus provides a contrast to the rich man of 18, 18–23 who cannot detach himself from his material possessions to become a follower of Jesus. Zacchaeus, according to Luke, exemplifies the proper attitude toward wealth: he promises to give half of his possessions to the poor (8) and consequently is the recipient of salvation (9–10).

19, 9: *A descendant of Abraham:* literally, "a son of Abraham." The tax collector Zacchaeus, whose repentance is attested by his determination to amend his former ways, shows himself to be a true descendant of Abraham, the true heir to the promises of God in the Old Testament. Underlying Luke's depiction of Zacchaeus as a descendant of Abraham, the father of the Jews (1, 73; 16, 22–31), is his recognition of the central place occupied by Israel in the plan of salvation.

19, 10: This verse sums up for Luke his depiction of the role of Jesus as savior in this gospel.

19, 11–27: In this parable Luke has combined two originally distinct parables: (1) a parable about the conduct of faithful and productive servants (13.15b–26) and (2) a parable about a rejected king (12.14–15a.27). The story about the conduct of servants occurs in another form in Mt 25, 14–20. The story about the rejected king may have originated with a contemporary historical event. After the death of Herod the Great, his son Archelaus traveled to Rome to receive the title of king. A delegation of Jews appeared in Rome before Caesar Augustus to oppose the request of Archelaus. Although not given the title of king, Archelaus was made ruler over Judea and Samaria. As the story is used by Luke, however, it furnishes a correction to the expectation of the imminent end of the age and of the establishment of the kingdom in Jerusalem (11). Jesus is not on his way to Jerusalem to receive the kingly power; for that, he must go away and only after returning from the distant country (a reference to the parousia) will reward and judgment take place.

19, 13: *Ten gold coins:* literally, "ten minas." A mina was a monetary unit that in ancient Greece was the equivalent of one hundred drachmas.

19, 28—21, 38: With the royal entry of Jesus into Jerusalem, a new section of Luke's gospel begins, the ministry of Jesus in Jerusalem before his death and resurrection. Luke suggests that this was a lengthy ministry in Jerusalem (19, 47; 20, 1; 21, 37–38; 22, 53) and it is characterized by Jesus' daily teaching in the temple (21, 37–38). For the story of the entry of Jesus into Jerusalem, see also Mt 21, 1–11; Mk 11, 1–10; Jn 12, 12–19 and the notes there.

19, 38: *Blessed is the king who comes in the name of the Lord:* only in Lk is Jesus explicitly given the title *king* when he enters Jerusalem in triumph. Luke has inserted this title into the words of Ps 118, 26 that heralded the arrival of the pilgrims coming to the holy city and to the temple. Jesus is thereby acclaimed as *king* (see 1, 32) and as the one *who comes* (see Mal 3, 1; Lk 7, 19). *Peace in heaven . . . :* the acclamation of the disciples of Jesus in Lk echoes the announcement of the angels at the birth of Jesus (2, 14). The peace Jesus brings is associated with the salvation to be accomplished here in Jerusalem.

19, 39: *Rebuke your disciples:* this command, found only in Lk, was given so that the Roman authorities would not interpret the acclamation of Jesus as king as an uprising against them; cf 23, 2–3.

19, 41–44: The lament for Jerusalem is found only in Lk. By not accepting Jesus (the one who mediates peace), Jerusalem will not find peace but will become the victim of devastation.

19, 43–44: Luke may be describing the actual disaster that befell Jerusalem in A.D. 70 when it was destroyed by the Romans during the First Revolt.

19, 45–46: Immediately upon entering the holy city, Jesus in a display of his authority enters the temple (see Mal 3, 1–3) and lays claim to it after cleansing it that it might become a proper place for his teaching ministry in Jerusalem (19, 47; 20, 1; 21, 37; 22, 53). See Mt 21, 12–17; Mk 11, 15–19; Jn 2, 13–17 and the notes there.

†Chapter Twenty Footnotes

20, 1–47: The Jerusalem religious leaders or their representatives, in an attempt to incriminate Jesus with the Romans and to discredit him with the people, pose a number of questions to him (about his authority, 2; about payment of taxes, 22; about the resurrection, 28–33).

20, 9–19: This parable about an absentee landlord and a tenant farmers' revolt reflects the social and economic conditions of rural Palestine in the first century. The synoptic gospel writers use the parable to describe how the rejection of the landlord's son becomes the occasion for the vineyard to be taken away from those to whom it was entrusted (the religious leadership of Judaism that rejects the teaching and preaching of Jesus; 19).

20, 15: *They threw him out of the vineyard and killed him:* cf Mk 12, 8. Luke has altered his Marcan source and reports that the murder of the son takes place outside the vineyard to reflect the tradition of Jesus' death outside the walls of the city of Jerusalem (see Heb 13, 12).

20, 20: *The governor:* i.e., Pontius Pilate, the Roman administrator responsible for the collection of taxes and maintenance of order in Palestine.

20, 22: Through their question the agents of the Jerusalem religious leadership hope to force Jesus to take sides on one of the sensitive political issues of first-century Palestine. The issue of nonpayment of taxes to Rome becomes one of the focal points of the First Jewish Revolt (A.D. 66–70) that resulted in the Roman destruction of Jerusalem and the temple. See also the note on Mt 22, 15–22.

20, 24: *Denarius:* a Roman silver coin (see the note on 7, 41).

20, 27: *Sadducees:* see the note on Mt 3, 7.

20, 28–33: The Sadducees' question, based on the law of levirate marriage recorded in Dt 25, 5–10, ridicules the idea of the resurrection. Jesus rejects their naive understanding of the resurrection (35–36) and then argues on behalf of the resurrection of the dead on the basis of the written law (37–38) that the Sadducees accept. See also the notes on Mt 22, 23–33.

20, 36: *Because they are the ones who will rise:* literally, "being sons of the resurrection."

20, 41–44: After successfully answering the three questions of his opponents, Jesus now asks them a question. Their inability to respond implies that they have forfeited their position and authority as the religious leaders of the people because they do not understand the scriptures. This series of controversies between the religious leadership of Jerusalem and Jesus reveals Jesus as the authoritative teacher whose words are to be listened to (see 9, 35). See also the notes on Mt 22, 41–46.

*Chapter Twenty References

20, 1–8:	Mt 21, 23–27; Mk 11, 27–33.	20:	11, 54.
2:	Acts 4, 7.	21:	Jn 3, 2.
4:	3, 3.16.	25:	Rom 13, 6–7.
5:	Mt 21, 32.	27–40:	Mt 22, 23–33; Mk 12, 18–27.
9–19:	Mt 21, 33–46; Mk 12, 1–12.	27:	Acts 23, 8.
9:	Is 5, 1–7.	28:	Gn 38, 8; Dt 25, 5.
10–12:	2 Chr 36, 15–16.	37:	Ex 3, 2.6.15–16.
13:	3, 22.	38:	Rom 14, 8–9.
17:	Ps 118, 22; Is 28, 16.	40:	Mt 22, 46; Mk 12, 34.
19:	19, 47–48; 22, 2; Mt 21, 46; Mk 11, 18; 12, 12; 14, 1–2; Jn 5, 18; 7, 30.	41–44:	Mt 22, 41–45; Mk 12, 35–37.
		42–43:	Ps 110, 1.
		45–47:	11, 37–54; Mt 23, 1–36; Mk 12, 38–40.
20–26:	Mt 22, 15–22; Mk 12, 13–17.	46:	14, 7–11.

*Chapter Twenty-One References

21, 1–4:	Mk 12, 41–44.	21:	17, 31.
5–6:	Mt 24, 1–2; Mk 13, 1–2.	23:	1 Cor 7, 26.
6:	19, 44.	24:	Tb 14, 5; Ps 79, 1; Is 63, 18; Jer 21, 7; Rom 11, 25; Rv 11, 2.
7–19:	Mt 24, 3–14; Mk 13, 3–13.		
8:	17, 23; Mk 13, 5.6.21; 1 Jn 2, 18.	25–28:	Mt 24, 29–31; Mk 13, 24–27.
10:	2 Chr 15, 6; Is 19, 2.	25:	Wis 5, 22; Is 13, 10; Ez 32, 7; Jl 2, 10; 3, 3–4; 4, 15; Rv 6, 12–14.
12–15:	12, 11–12; Mt 10, 17–20; Mk 13, 9–11.		
12:	Jn 16, 2; Acts 25, 24.	26:	Hg 2, 6.21.
15:	Acts 6, 10.	27:	Dn 7, 13–14; Mt 26, 64; Rv 1, 7.
16–18:	Mt 10, 21–22.	28:	2, 38.
16:	12, 52–53.	29–33:	Mt 24, 32–35; Mk 13, 28–31.
18:	12, 7; 1 Sm 14, 45; Mt 10, 30; Acts 27, 34.	32:	9, 27; Mt 16, 28.
		33:	16, 17.
19:	8, 15.	34:	12, 45–46; Mt 24, 48–50; 1 Thes 5, 3.6–7.
20–24:	Mt 24, 15–21; Mk 13, 14–19.		
20–22:	19, 41–44.	36:	Mk 13, 33.
		37:	19, 47; 22, 39.

†Chapter Twenty-One Footnotes

21, 1–4: The widow is another example of the poor ones in this gospel whose detachment from material possessions and dependence on God leads to their blessedness (6, 20). Her simple offering provides a striking contrast to the pride and pretentiousness of the scribes denounced in the preceding section (20, 45–47). The story is taken from Mk 12, 41–44.

21, 5–36: Jesus' eschatological discourse in Lk is inspired by Mk 13, but Luke has made some significant alterations to the words of Jesus found there. Luke maintains, though in a modified form, the belief in the early expectation of the end of the age (see 27.28. 31.32.36), but, by focusing attention throughout the gospel on the importance of the day-to-day following of Jesus and by reinterpreting the meaning of some of the signs of the end from Mk 13, he has come to terms with what seemed to the early Christian community to be a delay of the parousia. Mark, for example, described the desecration of the Jerusalem temple by the Romans (Mk 13, 14) as the apocalyptic symbol (see Dn 9, 27; 12, 11) accompanying the end of the age and the coming of the Son of Man. Luke (21, 20–24), however, removes the apocalyptic setting and separates the historical destruction of Jerusalem from the signs of the coming of the Son of Man by a period that he refers to as "the times of the Gentiles" (21, 24). See also the notes on Mt 24, 1–36 and Mk 13, 1–37.

21, 8: *The time has come:* in Lk, the proclamation of the imminent end of the age has itself become a false teaching.

21, 12: *Before all this happens . . . :* to Luke and his community, some of the signs of the end just described (10–11) still lie in the future. Now in dealing with the persecution of the disciples (12–19) and the destruction of Jerusalem (20–24) Luke is pointing to eschatological signs that have already been fulfilled.

21, 15: *A wisdom in speaking:* literally, "a mouth and wisdom."

21, 20–24: The actual destruction of Jerusalem by Rome in A.D. 70 upon which Luke and his community look back provides the assurance that, just as Jesus' prediction of Jerusalem's destruction was fulfilled, so too will be his announcement of their final redemption (27–28).

21, 24: *The times of the Gentiles:* a period of indeterminate length separating the destruction of Jerusalem from the cosmic signs accompanying the coming of the Son of Man.

21, 26: *The powers of the heavens:* the heavenly bodies mentioned in v 25 and thought of as cosmic armies.

*Chapter Twenty-Two References

22, 1–2:	Mt 26, 1–5; Mk 14, 1–2; Jn 11, 47–53.	33:	22, 54.
		34:	22, 54–62.
2:	19, 47–48; 20, 19; Mt 21, 46; Mk 12, 12; Jn 5, 18; 7, 30.	35:	9, 3; 10, 4; Mt 10, 9–10; Mk 6, 7–9.
		36:	22, 49.
		37:	Is 53, 12.
3–6:	Mt 26, 14–16; Mk 14, 10–11; Jn 13, 2.27.	39–46:	Mt 26, 30.36–46; Mk 14, 26.32–42; Jn 18, 1–2.
3:	Acts 1, 17.		
7–13:	Mt 26, 17–19; Mk 14, 12–16.	40:	22, 46.
		41:	Heb 5, 7–8.
7:	Ex 12, 6.14–20.	42:	Mt 6, 10.
13:	19, 32.	46:	22, 40.
14–20:	Mt 26, 20.26–30; Mk 14, 17.22–26; 1 Cor 11, 23–25.	47–53:	Mt 26, 47–56; Mk 14, 43–50; Jn 18, 3–4.
		49:	22, 36.
16:	13, 29.	50:	Jn 18, 26.
19:	24, 30; Acts 27, 35.	52:	22, 37.
20:	Ex 24, 8; Jer 31, 31; 32, 40; Zec 9, 11.	53:	19, 47; 21, 37; Jn 7, 30; 8, 20; Col 1, 13.
21–23:	Ps 41, 10; Mt 26, 21–25; Mk 14, 18–21; Jn 13, 21–30.	54–62:	Mt 26, 57–58.69–75; Mk 14, 53–54.66–72; Jn 18, 12–18.25–27.
24:	9, 46; Mt 18, 1; Mk 9, 34.	54:	22, 33.
		61:	22, 34.
25–27:	Mt 20, 25–27; Mk 10, 42–44; Jn 13, 3–16.	63–65:	Mt 26, 67–68; Mk 14, 65.
		66–71:	Mt 26, 59–66; Mk 14, 55–64.
26:	Mt 23, 11; Mk 9, 35.	66:	Mt 27, 1; Mk 15, 1.
29:	12, 32.	67:	Jn 3, 12; 8, 45; 10, 24.
30:	Mt 19, 28.		
31–34:	Mt 26, 33–35; Mk 14, 29–31; Jn 13, 37–38.	69:	Ps 110, 1; Dn 7, 13–14; Acts 7, 56.
31:	Jb 1, 6–12; Am 9, 9.		

†Chapter Twenty-Two Footnotes

22, 1—23, 56a: The passion narrative. Luke is still dependent upon Mk for the composition of the passion narrative but has incorporated much of his own special tradition into the narrative. Among the distinctive sections in Lk are: (1) the tradition of the institution of the Eucharist (22, 15–20); (2) Jesus' farewell discourse (22, 21–38); (3) the mistreatment and interrogation of Jesus (22, 63–71); (4) Jesus before Herod and his second appearance before Pilate (23, 6–16); (5) words addressed to the women followers on the way to the crucifixion (23, 27–32); (6) words to the penitent thief (23, 39–41); (7) the death of Jesus (23, 46.47b–49). Luke stresses the innocence of Jesus (23, 4.14–15.22) who is the victim of the powers of evil (22, 3.31.53) and who goes to his death in fulfillment of his Father's will (22, 42.46). Throughout the narrative Luke emphasizes the mercy, compassion, and healing power of Jesus (22, 51; 23, 43) who does not go to death lonely and deserted, but is accompanied by others who follow him on the way of the cross (23, 26–31.49).

22, 1: *Feast of Unleavened Bread, called the Passover:* see the note on Mk 14, 1.

22, 3: *Satan entered into Judas:* see the note on 4, 13.

22, 10: *A man will meet you carrying a jar of water:* see the note on Mk 14, 13.

22, 15: *This Passover:* Luke clearly identifies this last supper of Jesus with the apostles as a Passover meal that commemorated the deliverance of the Israelites from slavery in Egypt. Jesus reinterprets the significance of the Passover by setting it in the context of the kingdom of God (16). The "deliverance" associated with the Passover finds its new meaning in the blood that will be shed (20).

22, 17: Because of a textual problem in vv 19 and 20, some commentators interpret this cup as the eucharistic cup.

22, 19c–20: *Which will be given . . . do this in memory of me:* these words are omitted in some important Western text manuscripts and a few Syriac manuscripts. Other ancient text types, including the oldest papyrus manuscript of Lk dating from the late second or early third century, contain the longer reading presented here. The Lucan account of the words of institution of the Eucharist bears a close resemblance to the words of institution in the Pauline tradition (see 1 Cor 11, 23–26). See also the notes on Mt 26, 26–29; 26, 27–28; and Mk 14, 22–24.

22, 24–38: The Gospel of Luke presents a brief farewell discourse of Jesus; compare the lengthy farewell discourses and prayer in Jn, chs 13–17.

22, 25: *'Benefactors':* this word occurs as a title of rulers in the Hellenistic world.

22, 31: All of you: literally, "you." The translation reflects the meaning of the Greek text that uses a second person plural pronoun here.

22, 31–32: Jesus' prayer for Simon's faith and the commission to strengthen his brothers anticipates the post-resurrectional prominence of Peter in the first half of Acts, where he appears as the spokesman for the Christian community and the one who begins the mission to the Gentiles (Acts 10–11).

22, 36: In contrast to the ministry of the Twelve and of the seventy-two during the period of Jesus (9, 3; 10, 4), in the future period of the church the missionaries must be prepared for the opposition they will face in a world hostile to their preaching.

22, 38: *It is enough!:* the farewell discourse ends abruptly with these words of Jesus spoken to the disciples when they take literally what was intended as figurative language about being prepared to face the world's hostility.

22, 43–44: These verses, though very ancient, were probably not part of the original text of Lk. They are absent from the oldest papyrus manuscripts of Lk and from manuscripts of wide geographical distribution.

22, 51: *And healed him:* only Luke recounts this healing of the injured servant.

22, 61: Only Luke recounts that *the Lord turned and looked at Peter.* This look of Jesus leads to Peter's weeping bitterly over his denial (62).

22, 66–71: Luke recounts one daytime trial of Jesus (66–71) and hints at some type of preliminary nighttime investigation (54–65). Mark (and Matthew who follows Mk) has transferred incidents of this day into the nighttime interrogation with the result that there appear to be two Sanhedrin trials of Jesus in Mk (and Mt); see the note on Mk 14, 53.

22, 66: *Sanhedrin:* the word is a Hebraized form of a Greek word meaning a "council," and refers to the elders, chief priests, and scribes who met under the high priest's leadership to decide religious and legal questions that did not pertain to Rome's interests. Jewish

sources are not clear on the competence of the Sanhedrin to sentence and to execute during this period.

*Chapter Twenty-Three References

23, 1–5: Mt 27, 1–2.11–14; Mk 15, 1–5; Jn 18, 28–38.	33: 22, 37; Is 53, 12.
2: 20, 22–25; Acts 17, 7; 24, 5.	34: Nm 15, 27–31; Ps 22, 19; Mt 5, 44; Acts 7, 60.
3: 22, 70; 1 Tm 6, 13.	35–36: Ps 22, 8–9.
4: 23, 14.22.41; Mt 27, 24; Jn 19, 4.6; Acts 13, 28.	35: 4, 23.
7: 3, 1; 9, 7.	36: Ps 69, 22; Mt 27, 48; Mk 15, 36.
8: 9, 9; Acts 4, 27–28.	41: 23, 4.14.22.
9: Mk 15, 5.	42: 9, 27; 23, 2.3.38.
10: Mt 27, 12; Mk 15, 3.	43: 2 Cor 12, 3; Rv 2, 7.
11: Mt 27, 28–30; Mk 15, 17–19; Jn 19, 2–3.	44–49: Mt 27, 45–56; Mk 15, 33–41; Jn 19, 25–30.
14: 23, 4.22.41.	44–45: Am 8, 9.
16: 23, 22; Jn 19, 12–14.	45: Ex 26, 31–33; 36, 35.
18–25: Mt 27, 20–26; Mk 15, 6–7.11–15; Jn 18, 38b-40; 19, 14–16;Acts 3, 13–14.	46: Ps 31, 6; Acts 7, 59.
26–32: Mt 27, 32.38; Mk 15, 21.27; Jn 19, 17.	48: 18, 13; Zec 12, 10.
28–31: 19, 41–44; 21, 23–24.	49: 8, 1–3; 23, 55–56; 24, 10; Ps 38, 12.
30: Hos 10, 8; Rv 6, 16.	50–56: Mt 27, 57–61; Mk 15, 42–47; Jn 19, 38–42; Acts 13, 29.
33–43: Mt 27, 33–44; Mk 15, 22–32; Jn 19, 17–24.	51: 2, 25.38.
	53: 19, 30; Acts 13, 29.
	55: 8, 2; 23, 49; 24, 10.
	56: Ex 12, 16; 20, 10; Dt 5, 14.

†Chapter Twenty-Three Footnotes

23, 1–5.13–25: Twice Jesus is brought before Pilate in Luke's account, and each time Pilate explicitly declares Jesus innocent of any wrongdoing (4.14.22). This stress on the innocence of Jesus before the Roman authorities is also characteristic of John's gospel (Jn 18 38; 19, 4.6). Luke presents the Jerusalem Jewish leaders as the ones who force the hand of the Roman authorities (1–2.5.10.13. 18.21.23–25).

23, 6–12: The appearance of Jesus before Herod is found only in this gospel. Herod has been an important figure in Lk (9, 7–9; 13, 31–33) and has been presented as someone who has been curious about Jesus for a long time. His curiosity goes unrewarded. It is faith in Jesus not curiosity, that is rewarded (7, 50; 8, 48.50; 17, 19).

23, 17: This verse, "He was obliged to release one prisoner for them at the festival," is not part of the original text of Lk. It is an explanatory gloss from Mk 15, (also Mt 27, 15) and is not found in many early and important Greek manuscripts. On its historical background, see the notes on Mt 27, 15–26.

23, 26–32: An important Lucan theme throughout the gospel has been the need for the Christian disciple to follow in the footsteps of Jesus. Here this theme comes to the fore with the story of Simon of Cyrene who takes up the cross and follows Jesus (see 9, 23; 14, 27) and with the large crowd who likewise follow Jesus on the way of the cross. See also the note on Mk 15, 21.

23, 34a: *[Then Jesus said, "Father, forgive them, they know not what they do."]:* this portion of v 34 does not occur in the oldest papyrus manuscript of Lk and in other early Greek manuscripts and ancient versions of wide geographical distribution.

23, 39–43: This episode is recounted only in this gospel. The penitent sinner receives salvation through the crucified Jesus. Jesus' words to the penitent thief reveal Luke's understanding that the destiny of the Christian is "to be with Jesus."

23, 44: *Noon . . . three in the afternoon:* literally, the sixth and ninth hours. See the note on Mk 15, 25.

23, 47: *This man was innocent:* or, "This man was righteous."

*Chapter Twenty-Four References

24, 1–8: Mt 28, 1–8; Mk 16, 1–8; Jn 20, 1–17.	**27:** 24, 44; Dt 18, 25; Ps 22, 1–18; Is 53; 1 Pt 1, 10–11.
4: 2 Mc 3, 26; Acts 1, 10.	**34:** 1 Cor 15, 4–5.
5: Acts 2, 9.	**36–53:** Mk 16, 14–19; Jn 20, 19–20.
7: 9, 22.44; 17, 25; 18, 32–33; Mt 16, 21; 17, 22–23; Mk 9, 31; Acts 17, 3.	**36:** 1 Cor 15, 5.
	37: Mt 14, 26.
8: Jn 2, 22.	**40–41:** Jn 21, 5.9–10.13.
9–11: Mk 16, 10–11; Jn 20, 18.	**42:** Acts 10, 41.
	44: 18, 31; 24, 27; Mt 16, 21; Jn 5, 39.46.
10: 8, 2–3; Mk 16, 9.	**45:** Jn 20, 9.
12: Jn 20, 3–7.	**46:** 9, 22; Is 53; Hos 6, 2.
13: Mk 16, 12–13.	
16: Jn 20, 14; 21, 4.	**47:** Mt 3, 2; 28, 19–20; Mk 16, 15–16; Acts 10, 41.
19: Mt 2, 23; 21, 11; Acts 2, 22.	
21: 1, 54.68; 2, 38.	**48:** Acts 1, 8.
22–23: 24, 1–11; Mt 28, 1–8; Mk 16, 1–8.	**49:** Jn 14, 26; Acts 1, 4; 2, 3–4.
24: Jn 20, 3–10.	**50–51:** Mk 16, 19; Acts 1, 9–11.
25–26: 9, 22; 18, 31; 24, 44; Acts 3, 24; 17, 3.	**52:** Acts 1, 12.

†Chapter Twenty-Four Footnotes

24, 1–53: The resurrection narrative in Lk consists of five sections: (1) the women at the empty tomb (23, 56b—24, 12); (2) the appearance to the two disciples on the way to Emmaus (24, 13–35); (3) the appearance to the disciples in Jerusalem (24, 36–43); (4) Jesus' final instructions (24, 44–49); (5) the ascension (24, 50–53). In Lk, all the resurrection appearances take place in and around Jerusalem; moreover, they are all recounted as having taken place on Easter Sunday. A consistent theme throughout the narrative is that the suffering, death, and resurrection of Jesus were accomplished in fulfillment of Old Testament promises and of Jewish hopes (19a.21.26–27.44.46). In his second volume, Acts, Luke will argue that Christianity is the fulfillment of the

hopes of Pharisaic Judaism and its logical development (see Acts 24, 10–21).

24, 6a: *He is not here, but he has been raised:* this part of the verse is omitted in important representatives of the Western text tradition, but its presence in other text types and the slight difference in wording from Mt 28, 6 and Mk 16, 6 argue for its retention.

24, 9: The women in this gospel do not flee from the tomb and tell no one, as in Mk 16, 8, but return and tell the disciples about their experience. The initial reaction to the testimony of the women is disbelief (11).

24, 12: This verse is missing from the Western textual tradition but is found in the best and oldest manuscripts of other text types.

24, 13–35: This episode focuses on the interpretation of scripture by the risen Jesus and the recognition of him in the breaking of the bread. The references to the quotations of scripture and explanation of it (25–27), the kerygmatic proclamation (34), and the liturgical gesture (30) suggest that the episode is primarily catechetical and liturgical rather than apologetic.

24, 13: *Seven miles:* literally, "sixty stades." A stade was 607 feet. Some manuscripts read "160 stades" or more than eighteen miles. The exact location of Emmaus is disputed.

24, 16: A consistent feature of the resurrection stories is that the risen Jesus was different and initially unrecognizable (37; Mk 16, 12; Jn 20, 14; 21, 4).

24, 26: *That the Messiah should suffer . . . :* Luke is the only New Testament writer to speak explicitly of a suffering Messiah (26.46; Acts 3, 18; 17, 3; 26, 23). The idea of a suffering Messiah is not found in the Old Testament or in other Jewish literature prior to the New Testament period, although the idea is hinted at in Mk 8, 31–33. See the notes on Mt 26, 63 and 26, 67–68.

24, 36–43.44–49: The Gospel of Luke, like each of the other gospels (Mt 28, 16–20; Mk 16, 14–15; Jn 20, 19–23), focuses on an important appearance of Jesus to the Twelve in which they are commissioned for their future ministry. As in vv 6 and 12, so in vv 36 and 40 there are omissions in the Western text.

24, 39–42: The apologetic purpose of this story is evident in the concern with the physical details and the report that Jesus ate food.

24, 46: See the note on 24, 26.

24, 49: *The promise of my Father:* i.e., the gift of the holy Spirit.

24, 50–53: Luke brings his story about the time of Jesus to a close with the report of the ascension. He will also begin the story of the time of the church with a recounting of the ascension. In the gospel, Luke recounts the ascension of Jesus on Easter Sunday night, thereby closely associating it with the resurrection. In Acts (1, 3.9–11; 13, 31) he historicizes the ascension by speaking of a forty-day period between the resurrection and the ascension. The Western text omits some phrases in vv 51 and 52, perhaps to avoid any chronological conflict with Acts 1 about the time of the ascension.

24, 53: The Gospel of Luke ends as it began (1, 9), in the Jerusalem temple.